Using the Remote to Channel Focus

The publishing team included Roxane Kadrlik Chlachula, development editor; Lorraine Kilmartin, reviewer; Shutterstock, cover image; prepress and manufacturing coordinated by the production departments of Saint Mary's Press.

The movie rating criteria from the United States Conference of Catholic Bishops (USCCB) on pages 9–10 is from the USCCB Office for Film and Broadcasting, at *www.usccb.org/movies/criteria.shtml*, accessed February 23, 2009. Copyright © USCCB. All rights reserved. Used with permission of the USCCB.

The bracketed excerpts discussing Fair Use guidelines on pages 10–11 are used with the permission of the Office for Catholic Youth Ministry of the Diocese of Wilmington, DE.

To view copyright terms and conditions for Internet materials cited here, log on to the home pages for the referenced Web sites.

During this book's preparation, all citations, facts, figures, names, addresses, telephone numbers, Internet URLs, and other pieces of information cited within were verified for accuracy. The authors and Saint Mary's Press staff have made every attempt to reference current and valid sources, but we cannot guarantee the content of any source, and we are not responsible for any changes that may have occurred since our verification. If you find an error in, or have a question or concern about, any of the information or sources listed within, please contact Saint Mary's Press.

Printed in the United States of America

3835

ISBN 978-1-59982-011-8

Using the Remote to Channel Jesus

50 Movie Clips for Ministry

Patrick J. Donovan

Saint Mary's Press®

Dedication

This book is dedicated to my wife, Maureen,

who always helps me see more clearly.

Contents

Introduction

Why Use Movies?

Young people today are more connected than most adults and have a better understanding of what is possible with technology than youth of a generation ago. Young people are well wired in this wireless world to connect with one another, their families, and their faith. To reach them, youth ministry leaders must be willing to go where young people are. In the case of this resource, this means sitting in front of a television or a movie screen.

This resource is designed to allow adults in ministry who wish to reach young people through film and television the possibility to engage those young people in meaningful conversations, activities, or prayer. Ever since I was a young person, I knew we could learn a lot from movies. We have learned, for instance, that you can see the Eiffel Tower from every hotel room in Paris and that all phone numbers in the United States start with 555. Watching *The Brady Bunch* taught me that when you are on television and you turn out the lights to go to bed, your bedroom will still be perfectly visible, just slightly bluish. Great action-adventure movies teach us that it is easy to land a plane if there is someone in the control tower to talk you down. Watch any movie or TV show where someone is in a car, and you will realize that even when driving down a perfectly straight road, it is necessary to turn the wheel vigorously from left to right every few moments.

Seriously, though, we do learn a great deal from movies (I use the term *movies* generically to mean not just movies but also television shows). Movies remind us about how precious life can be as we watch the actors on the screen tell a story that mirrors our own. The funeral scene in *Steel Magnolias* (1989, rated PG), for instance, is painfully real for anyone who has lost a child (or a parent or a sibling). *Father of the Bride* (1991, rated PG) tells the story from a parents' perspective of watching their children grow and change. In the end, the children still need to say good-bye to Mom and Dad as they leave for their honeymoon. The movie *Stepmom* (1998, rated PG-13) reminds us that blended families are still families. *Finding Nemo* (2003, rated G) teaches parents that even as we seek to protect our children, we may inadvertently lead them into danger. It teaches children that the words they speak to their parents can hurt them. *War Games* (1983, rated PG) shows us how big computers once were, but also that sometimes innocent games have the possibility of drastic consequences.

Movies have become society's way of telling the stories found in history books. Young people have learned about the sacrifices of war from epics like *Saving Private Ryan* (1998, rated R) and about the horrors of the holocaust from *Schindler's List* (1993, rated R). Even *Titanic* (1997, rated PG-13), though more a love story than a recounting of history, teaches about historic events.

So if young people are watching countless hours of movies and television, and if society is using this medium to interact with young people, it only makes sense that we too would use the remote to help channel Jesus into the young Church of today.

About the Sessions

The sessions in this book are based on fifty different films. The sessions are organized by the ratings assigned by the United States Conference of Catholic Bishops. Each page includes notes and instructions for using the particular film, so the pages are not intended to be photocopied and handed out to the young people.

Each page includes the title of the film, the name of the studio that released it at the theater (occasionally this differs from the studio that released it on DVD, especially with independent films), the year it was released, and the ratings. Both the United States Conference of Catholic Bishops (USCCB) rating (only movies rated A-I, A-II, or A-III are used) and the Motion Picture Association of America rating (only movies rated G, PG, or PG-13 are included, as are some that are not rated [NR] at all) are noted.

The "Suggested Use" is just that—a suggestion. Three designations are used: conversation starter, activity, and prayer. You may find that some activities work for more than one film or that a film that is not designated as part of a prayer service fits perfectly within the prayer you are preparing. Feel free to use the outlines in various ways as they fit with your ministry. In a few cases, an optional activity or prayer is indicated in addition to the suggested use.

At the back of the book is an index that indicates which movies are suggested to be used as activities, conversation starters or within the context of prayer.

The "Materials" section lists either "Just your basic setup" or that phrase plus a list of materials needed for the activity or prayer. You should know the size of the room you will be using and how to set up a DVD player and projector with speakers, if necessary. It is important to know how many young people will be attending the session. A 27-inch television works well for a group of about ten. If your group is larger than that, you may need to make other arrangements. A laptop connected to your basic projector (with speakers attached to the computer) will do the trick in most cases. A blank wall, or a sheet hanging on the wall, suffices as a surface for viewing.

The "Themes" section lists specific themes that apply to the selected scenes. The themes are organized in no particular order. The index at the back of the book is your best bet if you are shopping by theme as you prepare your sessions.

The "Length of Clip" section denotes the amount of time needed to show the clip. Most clips run between 5 and 8 minutes. Some are shorter and may need to be shown more than once. Others are longer. Some sessions include the option of letting the scene play out. This is covered more in the "Setting the Scene" section, which is detailed later in this introduction.

The start and stop instructions assume you are watching the film on DVD. If you are watching the film on videocassette, use the time codes to help you find the right start and stop points. If you are using a DVD, fast forward to the chapter indicated (or choose that chapter from the disc's menu). Some clips start at the beginning of the chapters, so you will be ready to go once you get to that chapter marker. In other cases, you may need to fast-forward to a more exact spot, using the time codes that are included. If you are using a VCR, the time code assumes you are counting from the start of the movie (excluding previews). To make it easier for you, a short description of the scene indicates what you should be looking for.

Setting the Scene

First, watch the movie—the whole movie. Second, watch it again (with different people, if possible). As you are watching, note what the suggested scene teaches you. Watch the scene several times to make sure you have the timing right. Go through the session, the questions, the activities, and the follow-up to make sure you have a good handle on this material. Ask yourself these questions: Can the scene speak for itself? How will I introduce it? Will my audience be moved to see the rest of the film? Then ask yourself these questions: What's next? How will I begin the conversation or prayer or activity?

Practice on someone outside the ministry world to see if he or she sees what you see. Perhaps this person will have a better idea of how to introduce the scene. Maybe he or she will see something you didn't see that might create a problem. It is especially important that you know your audience. You may not know every young person who walks through your door, but you should know your community well enough to know if a particular movie scene could be inappropriate. You would not use, for instance, the scene from *Raising Helen* (2004, rated PG-13) with a group that includes a young person who recently lost a parent, unless you were well prepared.

Being well prepared to lead is a sign of respect for the young people. This book assumes you will watch the movies and read over the sessions prior to using the scenes or the sessions. There is no script for you to follow in setting the scene for the young people. Watching the movie on your own or with friends will allow you to set the scene in your own words. I remember a parent who had seen *Finding Nemo* and only remembered she loved the film. She forgot that it begins with Nemo's mother getting eaten and so had to quickly turn the film off when her young children became scared. Another friend of mine took her early adolescents to see *Titanic* because she had not done her research and thought it was a documentary about the sinking of the great ship. Much to her dismay, the movie turned into a dysfunctional love story and included a steamy, not to mention out-of-wedlock, sex scene. So do yourself and your young people a favor and prepare well for your time with them.

The "Suggested Process" section was developed to help make your time with the young people run more smoothly. Set the scene with the young people, show the clip, and then facilitate a discussion about the scene you have used. Do not be afraid of silence, especially with powerful clips. Let the scene sit for a minute, and give the young people a chance to absorb its meaning. Then ask the first question.

After the discussion questions, which may include an activity, consider using the variation offered, if time allows. If you have two groups of young people—a junior high and a senior high group, for instance—you could use one variation with one group and another variation with the other.

Avoid Common Mistakes

The first mistake, of course, would be thinking you could just pick up a movie and show a clip, never having watched the film in its entirety. Another mistake would be failing to set the scene appropriately, leaving the young people to ask, "What has this got to do with anything?" In addition, be aware of using too much of a good thing. You may think the entire movie is powerful, but soon you may find yourself asking, "Why are all the kids asleep?" Young people have a limited attention span, so use that to your advantage. Stick to the scenes outlined here.

A common mistake is forgetting to prescreen a film. Some clips, although none are from R-rated movies, do include profanity. Be aware of that so you know how to deal with it.

Finally, do not forget that not everyone should see every film, no matter how much you like it. *Shawshank Redemption* (1994, rated R) is an excellent film, but is it for junior high? It is not included here, by the way. Recall the example of the young person who recently lost a parent. *Raising Helen* is probably not for him or her. At least not until you are prepared for the conversations that might follow.

A Word About Ratings

A movie or show that is rated NR is not rated at all. This includes documentaries, cartoons, television shows (rated when they are shown on TV but not when released on DVD), and movies that were released before the modern-day rating system was put into place.

Movies with a G rating are suitable for general audiences. This includes some animated feature films and family films. Many early Walt Disney movies were released under this rating.

Movies with a PG rating may contain some material not suitable for kids (profanity and violence) but do not include drug use or explicit sex. Parental guidance is suggested.

A PG-13 rating indicates that some material may not be suitable for children under age thirteen. Movies that include scenes of drug use require this rating, as do those with even a single use of a four-letter sexually derived expletive. No scenes selected for this book include this word.

As stated earlier, this book does not contain any movies with an R rating, not just because this rating indicates that anyone under age seventeen will require an accompanying adult or adult guardian when seeing the film but also because those movies would not be in keeping with the A-I, A-II, or A-III ratings of the USCCB. Movies with hard language, drug use, tough violence, nudity within sexual scenes, and adult situations require this rating. This is not to say that R-rated movies (like *Schindler's List,* for instance) have nothing to teach us, just that those movies would require a separate resource.

Movie Ratings and the Bishops Conference

This book includes only movies with the ratings listed here. According to the USCCB Web site, this is the criteria the Office of Film and Broadcasting uses to rate movies in these categories:

A-I: GENERAL PATRONAGE. Strictly speaking, this does not simply connote films that are "for" children, or films in which they would necessarily be interested. Rather, any film free from significant objectionable content might receive this classification. In the old Hollywood days, when it was assumed that virtually all mainstream films were acceptable for all audiences, many films with "adult" subject matter, like *Giant,* received this classification. Nowadays, with even the cleanest adult films containing at least one four-letter word, such examples are rare.

A-II: ADULTS AND ADOLESCENTS. Though a 13-year-old is technically an adolescent, the original intent of this classification was an endorsement for older teens. However, some ambiguity remains in this category, and the Office generally indicates whether the film is most appropriate for "older teens" or anyone over the age of thirteen. Films with nudity, overt sexual activity (even if implied), violence with bloodshed, and use of four-letter words are almost never allowed in the A-I or A-II categories. *Akeelah and the Bee*—an uplifting film about a girl who wins a spelling bee—is one exception. In the film, one schoolmate utters an expletive. Yet, *Akeelah* was deemed so appropriate and inspirational for young viewers, that the movie was classified A-I.

A-III: ADULTS. This can be a tricky category. Adult sensibilities run the gamut from a cosmopolitan readership with a wider tolerance for edgy subject matter to more sensitive moviegoers who find certain elements less palatable. We try to strike a balance between the two. Oftentimes, a worthy film is clearly "adult" in subject matter, but older teens might derive benefit from it, so a sentence may be added about it being "acceptable" or "possibly acceptable" for "older teens." Dramatically justified violence, moderate sexual content of a "nondeviant" nature, restrained nudity, and valid use of coarse language are permissible here.

What the Law Says About Showing Movies

The Federal Copyright Act (Title 17, United States Code, Public Law 94-553, 90 stat. 2541) governs how copyrighted materials, such as movies, may be used. Neither the rental nor the purchase of a videocassette or DVD carries with it the right to use the movie outside the home. The bracketed information that follows is from the Office for Catholic Youth Ministry of the Diocese of Wilmington and provides commentary to the law. It is used here with the permission of that office.

Section 5-23 "Fair Use"

In some instances, it is not required to obtain a Movie Copyright Compliance Site License when exhibiting copyrighted materials such as DVDs. There is a "face-to-face teaching exemption" that applies only to full-time non-profit educational institutions and only if: A teacher [or youth ministers/DRE, etc.] is in attendance and the showing takes place in a classroom setting [even a parish hall will suffice] and the movie is used as an essential part of the current curriculum being taught.

[According to the Motion Picture Licensing Association (MPLA), parochial schools and parishes affiliated with the schools are exempt from purchasing a site license so long as the above criteria are met. This means, for instance, that a youth minister or classroom catechist can show a movie or clip(s) of a movie as part of the educational process or in [a] ministry setting (and not solely for entertainment). Writing out the curriculum is recommended and adult leaders should be reminded that the law prohibits the use of pirated movies. Only an original is to be used in a classroom setting.]

Examples of situations where a Movie Copyright Compliance Site License must be obtained are public libraries, day-care facilities, and non-classroom entertainment movies being used at schools for after-school activities. This legal requirement applies: regardless of whether an admission fee is charged, whether the institution or organization is commercial or non-profit, and whether a federal or state agency is involved. [This part of the Copyright Code can present a problem for parishes and schools as it prohibits the use of movies for purely entertainment purposes. This would include showing movies on a bus while on a trip or at an after-school care program, as well as a "movie night" with no written curriculum, educational purpose, or oral evaluation or discussion of the event. To show movies or clip(s) of movies in such settings, a Site License should be purchased from the Motion Picture Licensing Corporation (*www.mplc.com*).]

In short, using this resource the way it was outlined is in keeping with the guidelines the MPLA offers and with the Fair Use guidelines, so long as a legal copy is used.

A Final Thought

Each session in this book includes some final thoughts from me. Some are my own thoughts on the scene I have recommended; others are comments in general. I hope you find these helpful.

The movies included in this book were chosen on purpose. Not all of them are new. In fact, only a few are from the last three or four years. The oldest is from 1966, and the newest is from 2007. If all we choose to use are the latest and most popular movies, we run the risk, I think, of teaching young people that only those films can teach us something. Some of the movies I use have probably never been seen by some adults. Some have been remade, but I use the original version, which young people have probably never seen. It is a nice mix of movies, if I do say so myself. Enjoy the show!

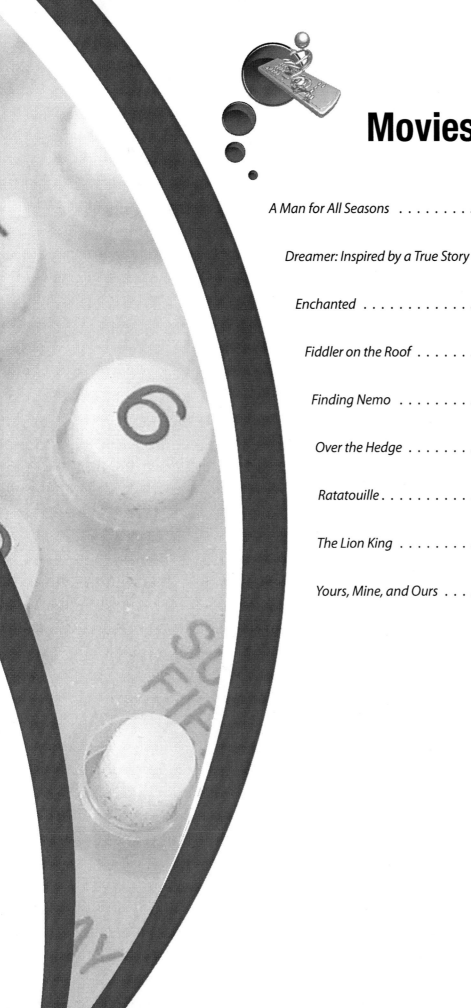

Movies Rated A-I

A Man for All Seasons

Highland Films, 1966, Rated A-I and G

SUGGESTED USE: Conversation Starter

MATERIALS: This film clip requires just your basic setup.

THEMES: Moral Decision Making, Conscience, True to Self, Peer Pressure

LENGTH OF CLIP: 07:16

> ▶ **Begin:** Chapter 23, 1:28:08 Begin as Sir Thomas is walking down the hall with the guards.

> ■ **End:** 1:35:24 End when Cromwell says, "We have to find another way."

Setting the Scene

Based on Robert Bolt's play of the same name, this film has been named one of the top twenty-five films by the Vatican. Telling the story of Saint Thomas More's refusal to accept King Henry VIII as the head of the Church in England, this masterpiece is a study in moral decision making. Faced with the possibility of being put to death, Sir Thomas goes willingly to jail rather than going against what he believes. Even when all his friends and colleagues have signed the Oath of Supremacy, he does not. He also refuses to tell why he will not sign the oath. In this scene, as Sir Thomas is questioned again, he tries to explain his silence to the Duke of Norfolk, once a close friend and advocate.

Suggested Process

 Show Clip

Discussion Questions

- Sir Thomas and the Duke of Norfolk were once close friends. Now the Duke has signed the oath and Sir Thomas has gone to jail. Do you think the Duke feels bad for his friend? Does he show it?

- At this point, Sir Thomas has been in prison in the Tower of London for years. Wouldn't it have been easier for him to just sign the oath and be released from prison? Why do you think he refuses?

- Have you ever believed in something so strongly that you were willing to stand alone to remain faithful to your beliefs? Have you ever known anyone else who was willing to do this?

- What do you think about Sir Thomas's response to the Duke about coming to hell "for fellowship"? How would you use such a line in your own situations at school, home, or work?

- In another scene, Sir Thomas's wife grows angry because he will not reveal his reasons for refusing to sign the oath. Instead he tells her: "In my silence is my safety, and my silence must be absolute." Why is silence often a good idea when it comes to having something to say about what other people are doing? When is silence not a good idea?

 ## Variation

Have the young people research the life of Sir Thomas More. Suggest they use the americancatholic.org Web site to access online information about the saint. The following questions provide direction for their research:

- What led to this point in Sir Thomas More's life?

- When was he canonized a saint?

- Is he the patron saint of any particular group of people?

- How did King Henry VIII come into power?

- How many times was he married, and how did those marriages affect the people of England?

 ## Final Thought

Use this clip as an opportunity to talk with the young people about peer pressure. The Duke of Norfolk simply wants his friend to sign the oath but fails to understand why that is asking too much of Sir Thomas More. The Duke and Sir Thomas More have been friends for a long time, and the Duke cannot understand why all other men of property have agreed to the oath. For Sir Thomas, it is a matter of conscience. He will not sign just because all the others have done so.

Ask the young people the following questions:

- What are you experiencing today that correlates to Sir Thomas More's situation?

- In what ways are you refusing to give in as a matter of conscience among your peers?

Dreamer: Inspired by a True Story

DreamWorks SKG, 2005, Rated A-I and PG

SUGGESTED USE: Conversation Starter

MATERIALS: This film clip requires just your basic setup, plus a Bible for the optional activity.

THEMES: Parent-Child Relationship, Family, Redemption, Parables

LENGTH OF CLIP: 04:37

▶	**Begin:**	Chapter 12, 0:55:53	Begin as Cale's father is sitting at the kitchen table.
■	**End:**	1:00:30	End after the conversation between Cale and her father.

Setting the Scene

Ben Crane lost his job when he refused, in front his young daughter, to euthanize a horse with a broken leg. He has also lost his business, and most of his farm, because his former boss has told others not to hire him. Now Ben thinks he has lost the respect of his family too. His daughter loves the horse—and her father—and in this scene, Ben learns that the two are connected.

Use this scene to discuss what may happen to the relationships between parents and their children when parents make a mistake. Encourage the young people to express their feelings to their parents, and help them to better understand what "respecting your mother and father" is all about.

Suggested Process

Show Clip

Discussion Questions

- Cale's father has lost his job, his business, most of his farm, and, he believes, the respect of his family. He attends parents' night at a point when he is about as low as he can be in his life. Why do you think we seem to learn the most during the difficult moments in life?

- As Ben reads his daughter's story, he realizes it is a parable about him. Why hasn't Cale come to her father directly to tell him how she feels?

- Have your parents ever had to admit their mistakes to you? Do you think that was an easy thing to do? Is it possible for children to "rescue" their parents? How?

- Why do you think it can be hard for family members to say "I love you"?

Variation

Ask the young people to think about what kind of parable would describe the parent-child relationship in their household. You could choose some parables from the Bible and ask the young people to try to find themselves in the stories. Here are some parables you might consider using:

- The Parable of the Lost Sheep (Luke 15:3–7, Matthew 18:12,13)
- The Parable of the Mustard Seed (Matthew 13:31–32, Mark 4:30–32)
- The Parable of the Sower (Matthew 13:1–23, Luke 8:4–18)
- The Parable of the Ten Bridesmaids (Matthew 25:1–13)
- The Parable of the Good Samaritan (Luke 10:25–37)
- The Parable of the House on the Rock (Matthew 7:12–29)
- The Parable of the Prodigal Son (Luke 15:11–32)

Final Thought

Remind the young people that every family has strife. Some face financial hardships, illness, or tragedy. Most families have, like Ben did, a family member with whom they do not get along. Invite the young people to think about the challenges their families are experiencing and how they might help to resolve those challenges.

Enchanted

Walt Disney, 2007, Rated A-I and PG

SUGGESTED USE: Activity with an Optional Prayer

MATERIALS: This film clip requires just your basic setup, plus an index card and a pen or pencil for each young person, a sheet of newsprint and a marker, and a roll of tape.

THEMES: Love, Marriage, Kindness, Relationships

LENGTH OF CLIP: 07:12

> ▶ **Begin:** Chapter 10, 0:45:24   Begin as Giselle and Robert walk along the path.

> ⏹ **End:**   0:52:36   End after the song is finished.

Setting the Scene

Robert cannot understand why Giselle is always so happy or how she can believe so naively in love and happily ever after. This scene follows the one where Robert has tried to get rid of Giselle, telling her to go away. Drawn to her innocence, Robert is not able to leave her quickly, so they walk in the park and Giselle talks about what it means to show someone you care about him or her.

Use this scene to introduce the activity, which asks the young people to first identify the number of ways Giselle and the crowd speak of showing kindness. Then invite the young people to write down ways they can show their love for others.

Suggested Process

 Show Clip

Discussion Questions

- Robert says that "happily ever after" does not exist. Do you believe him? What do you think the secret is to a happy marriage?

- Robert says that he and Nancy know they love each other but do not need to talk about it all the time. Do you believe it is important to tell people how you feel about them? What about your friends? How do they know if you care for them? What about your parents? Do you think they want to hear you verbalize your love, or do you expect them to just know how you feel? What are the benefits of being told how others feel about you?

Activity

This activity has the young people listen to the song and identify the number of ways Giselle and the crowd speak of showing someone you love her or him. You might need to play the song more than once and turn on the subtitles to make the challenge a little easier. After the young people have identified the number of ways to show someone you love her or him, use the sheet of newsprint to list all the ways that were mentioned in the song. Depending on how you count, there are either fourteen or fifteen ways mentioned in the song. Post the sheet of newsprint on a wall where everyone can see it.

Distribute the index cards and the pens or pencils to the young people and ask them to each write down the names of five people in their lives. Then have them write, next to each name, a way they can show that person they love her or him.

When everyone is done, ask the young people to each share with the group the names of one or two of the people on their list and the ways they have come up with to express their love for those people. Keep a list of names the young people share with the group and save it to use for the closing prayer.

Optional Prayer

Use the list of names that the young people shared with the group as spoken intentions in a closing prayer.

Final Thought

Before you close, inquire as to whether prayer was listed as one of the ways we can express love. For some on our lists, it might be the best way to express our care and concern for them.

Fiddler on the Roof

MGM, 1971, Rated A-I and G

SUGGESTED USE: Activity

MATERIALS: This film clip requires just your basic setup.

THEMES: Love, Marriage

LENGTH OF CLIP: 04:52

▶ **Begin:** Chapter 26, 2:03:53 Begin as Tevye enters the house.

◼ **End:** 2:08:45 End as the song concludes and the scene fades to black.

Setting the Scene

This is a movie classic that most young people have never seen on the big screen. In this particular scene, Tevye has just met his daughter and her boyfriend along the road. The couple has asked for his blessing to be married, and he has given it to them. Tevye returns home and tells his wife, Golde, that he has just given his blessing for his dauther to get married. Golde becomes irate since the man to whom her daughter is now engaged has little money and no apparent way of supporting either himself or his bride-to-be. Times are difficult in the town, and one daughter has already been married. As with most parents, Tevye and his wife want only the best for their children. In this case, it means having their daughters marry men who can provide for them. Sometimes, however, love enters in and our plans become irrelevant.

Suggested Process

Show Clip

 **Activity**

Invite the young people to gather in a circle. Then offer the following instructions:

- We are going to go around the circle, each one of us taking a turn to complete a sentence. Listen carefully for the way the sentence is worded so you know how to complete it. I will begin the activity. "I love . . . *[Insert the name of someone you know well, such as a parent, a spouse, or one of your children].*"

After everyone has had a turn completing the first sentence, pause and start again with the second sentence. There are a total of five variations of this sentence that the young people will expand on.

- We will go around the circle again, this time completing the sentence "I love *[insert the name of the same person as before]* because . . ." Be sure to name the same person as you named in the first round. When everyone has had a turn, continue with the third sentence:

- This time around the sentence is "I love *[same person]* and so I . . ." Name something you do for that person to show you love him or her. When everyone has had a turn, continue with the fourth sentence:

- This time around the sentence is "I know God loves me because . . ." When everyone has had a turn, continue with the fifth sentence:

- The last time around, the sentence is "I love God, so I will . . ."

 Final Thought

Conclude this activity with a prayer. When you are finished with round five, simply ask, "For what else shall we pray?" Close with a prayer "for the people we have named and the strength to do the things we have named for those we love."

Finding Nemo

Walt Disney/Pixar, 2003, Rated A-I and G

SUGGESTED USE: Conversation Starter

MATERIALS: This film clip requires just your basic setup.

THEMES: Parenting, Respect, Peer Pressure, Disabilities

LENGTH OF CLIP: 08:06

▶ **Begin:**   Chapter 3, 0:05:18   Begin as Nemo wakes up, excited to go to school.

■ **End:**   0:13:24   End after Nemo tells his father he hates him.

Setting the Scene

This modern-day classic about a father's love for his child is a great story about the need to give children their independence and space. This particular clip occurs at the beginning of the movie, when Nemo says something to his father that many kids say at some point—something a father never wants to hear.

Suggested Process

 Show Clip

Discussion Questions

- Why does Nemo get so upset when his father just wants to protect him? Why are parents sometimes overprotective?

- At the beginning of the film, Nemo's mother and siblings die. What effect can the death of someone close have on the relationships between parents and children?

- Have you ever told your parents you hate them? How did they react? Do you think it hurt their feelings?

- How can you express frustration with your parents without hurting their feelings?

 ## Variation

This is a great clip to use at a parents meeting to introduce a discussion about the parent-child relationship as it relates to the faith development of teens. For instance, you might suggest that on the way home, the parents talk with their teens about the relationship they had with their own parents. What were the high points? the low points? Did they ever see their parents struggle with their faith? You might also suggest that the parents share with their teens some of the struggles they have encountered in their own relationship with God. The young people will be better off for having shared in a conversation that includes some honest dialogue between them and their parents.

 ## Final Thought

Discuss with the young people what they think it does to parents when they hear their own son or daughter say, "I hate you," or similar words. Reiterate that the words we speak can be quite powerful.

Ask the young people the following questions:

- What are the implications of this movie clip for your relationship with your parents?

- Are there words you wish you had not spoken, things you wish you had never said? If so, what lessons can you find among those words?

Over the Hedge

DreamWorks, 2006, Rated A-I and PG

SUGGESTED USE: Activity

MATERIALS: This film clip requires just your basic setup, plus a sheet of paper and a pen or pencil for each small group of four.

THEMES: Conservation, Gluttony, Materialism

LENGTH OF CLIP: 03:30

▶ **Begin:** Chapter 5, 0:18:56 Begin when R. J. announces, "Welcome to suburbia."

■ **End:** 0:22:26 End when Verne says, "Just a figure of speech."

Setting the Scene

R. J. is a racoon with a plan. In needing to replenish a stash of food, he convinces an unlikely (and slightly mixed-up) family of forest animals to help. In this scene, R. J. tries to impress his new friends with his knowledge of what's over the hedge—a new neighborhood that sprang up while the gang was hibernating. The scene provides some fantastic social commentary about life outside the big city and will allow the young people to take a good look at what they have in the way of material goods—and perhaps what they could do without.

Suggested Process

 Show Clip

Discussion Questions

- Earlier in the day, Verne had gone over the hedge and returned home describing a much scarier picture than what R. J. describes for the gang. What surprised you most about R. J.'s description of life in suburbia?

- R. J. comments that humans are slowly losing the ability to walk, so they buy massive SUVs, which usually hold only one person. Is there a lesson here? Are we unable to walk everywhere because of the ways we build our cities and neighborhoods, or do we build our cities and neighborhoods the way we do because no one really wants to walk anywhere?

- R. J. tells the gang: "We eat to live. These guys live to eat." Do you think that is true? What characteristics of our society support or don't support your answer?

- As R. J. goes through his monologue about humans and their love affair with food, we see a family in prayer. R. J. says, "That is the altar where they worship food." Is that a fair statement? Think about the prayer you say before meals. What do the words really mean to you?

- What does the comment "For humans, enough is never enough" mean? Is that a fair indictment about humans? Is it unique for our country, or is it more of a universal statement?

 ## Activity

Divide the large group into pairs. Present the following situation and question:

- Imagine that there is an earthquake *[or fire or flood, depending on where you live and how sensitive you need to be to your audience]* and you have only 5 minutes to get out of the house. Assume that family and pets are already safe. What possessions would you take with you?

When all the young people have had a chance to share with their partners, have the participants form small groups of four. Distribute a sheet of paper and a pen or pencil to each small group, and then offer the following directions:

- In your small groups, create a list of some of the things you did not take with you.

- Pick five things from that list that you could do without.

 ## Final Thought

After the young people have completed the task, challenge them to consider giving these things away or, even better, to forego collecting more things like this in the future. Challenge them to think about how they can say "enough" in their lives, so that those who have less than us might benefit.

Ratatouille

Walt Disney/Pixar, 2007, Rated A-I and G

SUGGESTED USE: Activity

MATERIALS: This film clip requires just your basic setup, plus paper plates and pens or pencils, one of each for each young person.

THEMES: Family, Self-Image, Honesty

LENGTH OF CLIP: 08:26

> ▶ **Begin:** Chapter 27, 1:32:27 Begin as Remy's father whistles.
>
> ⏹ **End:** 1:40:53 End when Linguini finishes reading the review in the newspaper.

Setting the Scene

Remy's family comes to the rescue, and Ego the food critic is in for a surprise. By his own admission, Ego says it is easier to criticize people than to admit that others are capable of great talent. Perhaps therein lies the lesson of this moral tale. Faithfulness to one's own self can lead to greatness around us. Recognizing that greatness, however, often involves a struggle and, more often than not, requires another's perspective. We often cannot see that which is so close to us.

Use this scene as an opportunity to have the participants affirm one another as they each recognize the greatness around them.

Suggested Process

 Show Clip

Discussion Questions

- Remy and Linguini serve ratatouille to Ego. It is a peasant dish that would ordinarily not be in keeping with such an upscale restaurant. Why do you think this simple act is so important to Ego?

- Linguini and Colette come clean and tell Ego that Remy is the brains behind the operation. Why is it so important for them, especially Linguini, to finally be honest?

- Ego has made a living criticizing others. He admits that it is nice to have such power over people and that negative criticism is fun to write and read. Why is it sometimes easier to be critical of people than to be kind?

- Ego says that "the bitter truth we critics must face is that in the grand scheme of things, the average piece of junk is probably more meaningful than our criticism designating it so." What do you think this means? What are the implications for such a statement in other areas of our lives? Why are we sometimes so ready to hand power over to people when they treat us unkindly?

- Ego reminds his readers that great talent can come from anywhere. Do you believe this is true? What is the great talent hidden among your group of friends? What gifts do you see in others?

 Activity

Distribute a paper plate and a pen or pencil to each young person. Ask them to write their name on their plates. When they are finished, ask them to pass the plates around the circle. As each participant receives a new plate, she or he should take a moment to write an affirming note to the person whose plate they are holding. Ask them to think about the qualities they admire in the person. Be sure each participant writes a note on each plate so that everyone gets a chance to affirm everyone else and be affirmed by everyone else. Remind the young people that Ego, by his own admission, says it is easier to criticize people than to admit that others are capable of great talent. Emphasize that the lesson in this moral tale is the importance of affirming others.

 Variation

Let the scene continue to play so the young people see that the restaurant ends up closing and everyone loses their jobs, including the food critic, who spoke so highly of Remy. In the end, they all join forces to open a new restaurant, and Remy is able to be true to himself, with a proud family standing by his side.

 Final Thought

Emphasize to the young people that this scene illustrates how it can sometimes be fun to be mean. It is sometimes fun to say or write words that are unkind. It is much easier than seeing Christ in others, yet we are all created in the image of Christ. How do you see Christ in others?

The Lion King

Walt Disney, 1994, Rated A-I and G

SUGGESTED USE: Conversation Starter

MATERIALS: This film clip requires just your basic setup.

THEMES: Baptism, New Life, Parent-Child Relationship

LENGTH OF CLIP: 03:57

▶ **Begin:** Chapter 1, 0:00:30   Begin with either the opening credits, or fast-forward to the sunrise and the beginning of the song.

⏹ **End:** 0:04:27   End when the song ends and the title hits the screen.

Setting the Scene

In this scene, the animal community comes together and witnesses a blessing, an anointing, a Baptism, and a prayer. The community rejoices together at the presentation of Simba, the lion cub.

Use this scene to help young people understand the sacraments of initiation. Point out the parallels between this scene and the anointing at Baptism and Confirmation, being held by your parents at Baptism and supported by your sponsor at Confirmation, being presented to the community at Baptism and having the community rejoice that you are present and joined with them in faith at Confirmation.

Suggested Process

 Show Clip

Discussion Questions

- How many of you have seen this film before? How many of you have seen the story acted out in the theater? What is happening in this scene?

- How many of you have seen a Baptism take place at church? How is this scene reflective of what happens during a Baptism? Specifically, what are the rituals we perform when a young person or adult is baptized? What are the rituals performed in this scene? How many can you name? Are there any that are similar to one another?

- Why do the animals bow down when the rays of the sun shine on Simba? Are they respecting the king's new son or the King?

- Why do you think the animals seem to be rejoicing more than human beings do at a child's Baptism? What are they celebrating with such joy?

- Why do you think the song "The Circle of Life" was written for this scene? What do the words mean to you? How do you experience the circle of life?

 ## Variation

Read the story of the baptism of Jesus in Matthew, chapter 3. Invite the young people to name the similarities between the Scripture passage and the film clip. Compare this Scripture passage with the versions in John, chapter 1; Mark, chapter 1; and Luke, chapter 3. Ask the participants to compare and discuss the stories in Scriptures.

 ## Final Thought

If you feel comfortable doing so, share with the young people an experience you have had with the "circle of life."

Yours, Mine, and Ours

MGM, 1968, Rated A-I and NR

SUGGESTED USE: Activity

MATERIALS: This film clip requires just your basic setup, plus sheets of newsprint and markers, one of each for each small group of four or five.

THEMES: Human Sexuality, Family, Marriage, Love, Commitment

LENGTH OF CLIP: 05:27

▶ **Begin:** Chapter 15, 1:38:16   Begin when the house comes into view and Frank Beardsley starts talking.

⏹ **End:** 1:43:43   End as Frank and Helen drive to the hospital.

Setting the Scene

This movie, made in the late 1960s, explores the true-story antics of two families, with a load of children, that come together as one. This is one of the best clips to use in discussing human sexuality, marriage, and love. Frank and Helen are having their first child together at the same time their eldest daughter is struggling under the pressure of her boyfriend to become sexually active. You may have to show the clip more than once to be able to complete the activity.

Suggested Process

 Show Clip

Activity

Divide the large group into small groups of four or five. Distribute a sheet of newsprint and a marker to each small group, and then present the following directions:

- Recall the many ways Frank tells his daughter what love means. List them on the newsprint.

Explain that this movie was made more than forty years ago. Ask the young people the following questions:

- Do you think your lists are accurate today? What, if anything, would you add to this list to make it more up to date?

- Can you think of additional reasons to refrain from becoming sexually active before marriage? Try to come up with at least five original ideas and record them on your newsprint.

Variation

Have the young people spend some time researching what the Church teaches about chastity. Encourage them to read *Real Love: Answers to Your Questions on Dating, Marriage, and the Real Meaning of Sex,* by Mary Beth Bonacci (Fort Collins, CO: Ignatius Press, 1996), or *If You Really Loved Me: 100 Questions on Dating, Relationships, and Sexual Purity,* by Jason Evert (Cincinnati: Saint Anthony Messenger Press / Franciscan Communications, 2003), to learn more about love, human sexuality, and marriage.

Final Thought

Invite the young people to imagine themselves ten to fifteen years in the future. Ask the following question:

- If you were a parent and your children had questions about human sexuality, how would you approach the subject?

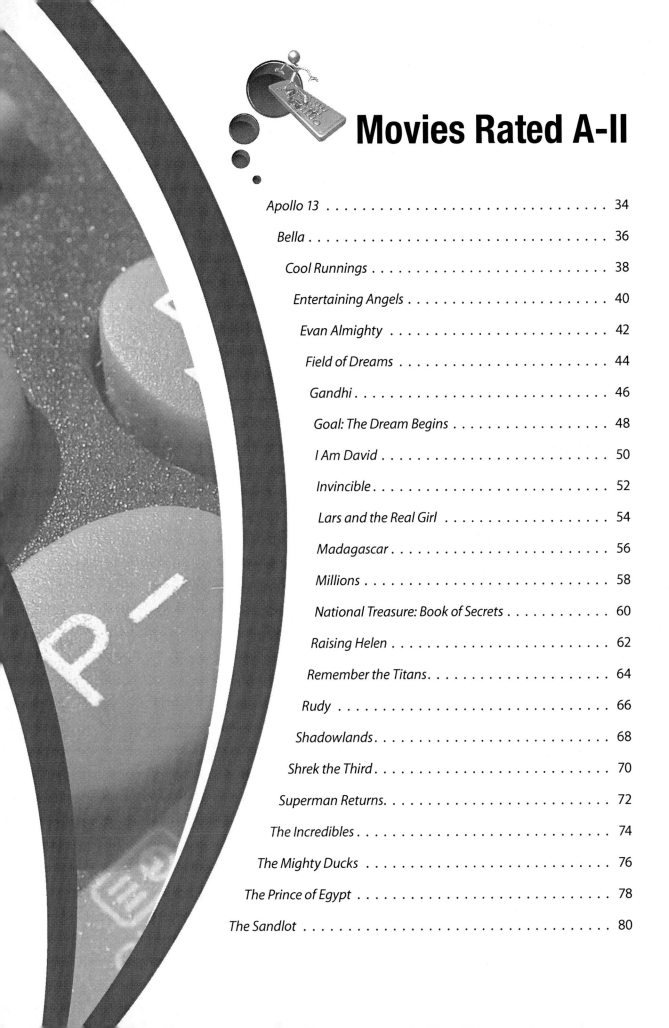

Movies Rated A-II

Apollo 13

Universal, 1995, Rated A-II and PG

SUGGESTED USE: Activity

MATERIALS: This film clip requires just your basic setup, plus a large paper grocery bag for each small group of four or five, with items such as aluminum cans, small paper bags, a small basket, some string, a play telephone, some sheets of paper, and a small flower pot. The only must-have item for each group's bag is either a rope or a swimming pool noodle (these provide the most fun). No two bags should be alike.

THEMES: Teamwork, Creativity

LENGTH OF CLIP: 01:25

> **Begin:** Chapter 35, 1:19:35   Begin as one of the engineers enters the room where many others are sleeping on the floor.

> **End:** 1:21:00   End after all the supplies are thrown on the table and the men start talking.

Setting the Scene

This epic tale about the doomed Apollo 13 mission gave a new generation an appreciation for technology, space travel, and a real understanding of "Houston, we have a problem." In this scene, the engineers have to solve a problem, and they have to do it quickly. The astronauts are running out of clean air, and the air filters from one system do not fit into another.

Use this scene to encourage the young people to creatively accomplish a task that at first may seem difficult and confusing.

Suggested Process

 Show Clip

 **Activity**

The idea here is that the young people, in their small groups, use their imagination and creativity to hatch their rescue plan. If you give too many instructions, you risk telling the groups what to do. If you are too vague, you risk frustrating the young people into doing nothing at all. It is a fine line, so walk carefully.

Divide the large goup into small groups of four or five and present the following directions:

- Suppose you are the engineers at NASA and you have been charged with rescuing the astronauts. Using only the supplies you have been given—and the creativity of your group—make a plan to rescue the team from outerspace.

When the small groups are done planning, allow them to present their rescue plans to the large group. Congratulate them on their creativity and then follow up with the discussion questions that follow.

 Discussion Questions

- What assets did your group discover they had that were not in the bag? How were these assets helpful in solving the task?
- Can you think of some tasks you might face at home or at school that could seem impossible at first? Are there any lessons from this clip or this activity that might be helpful in those situations?

 Variation

You could use this activity as a challenge between the young people and their parents. Be sure to give the adults intentionally vague instructions. Then sit back and enjoy the show.

 Final Thought

Ask the young people to think about the correlations between our own lives and this experience. Many situations in life do not include instructions; we must figure things out as we go. Ask the young people the following questions:

- Can you think of a time when life threw you a curveball and you had to try to hit it?
- What role did faith play as you prepared to swing?

Bella

Lions Gate, 2006, Rated A-II and PG-13

SUGGESTED USE: Activity

MATERIALS: This filim clip requires just your basic setup, plus an index card and a pen or pencil for each young person.

THEMES: Moral Decision Making, Friendship, Pregnancy, Sanctity of Life

LENGTH OF CLIP: 05:16

▶ **Begin:** Chapter 6, 0:25:18 Begin as Nina and José enter the restaurant.

⏹ **End:** 0:30:34 End as Nina is held by José and begins to cry.

Setting the Scene

Tied for second place with *Juno* on the USCCB's top-ten list of movies of 2007, *Bella* is the story of José, a former soccer player, whose life takes an unexpected turn when he is kind to his coworker Nina. Nina is pregnant, and because she has been sick a few times (and late on the morning the scene takes place), she is fired from her waitressing job by Manny, José's brother. José spends the day talking to Nina, welcomes her into his home, and makes a decision that changes the lives of many. *Bella* is one of those movies you can watch with a youth group or class and unpack the lessons of the film for days.

Suggested Process

 Show Clip

Discussion Questions

- How many reasons does Nina give for not wanting to keep the baby? Discuss the validity of her reasons.

- What does José mean when he challenges Nina, telling her that she is not alone?

- Nina said the father of the child uses the phrase "getting it taken care of" to descibe an abortion. Do you think Nina is right in describing the attitude of men toward unplanned pregnancies? Why?

- Discuss the way José talks to Nina. Does he ask a lot of questions? Does he judge her decision to end the pregnancy? What is it about his reaction and the way he treats Nina that earns him the right to be heard in the end?

Activity

Distribute an index card and a pen or pencil to each young person and then present the following directions:

- Imagine you are José. What do you whisper in Nina's ear? What do you think José says to her? Do you think it makes her change her mind? Use your index cards to write down your end of the conversation in the clinic. When everyone has finished, we will share our ideas with one another.

It is important that you not tell the young people what happens in the rest of the story if the activity is to have significant meaning. Allow the participants to share their answers, and then offer a prayer of thanksgiving for God's great gift of life.

Variation

Avoid conversations about premarital sex or debates about abortion. Instead use this scene as an opportunity to discuss the ways we react when someone does or says something we disagree with. Are we judgmental, or do we listen compassionately like José in this scene? How does the way we react to others affect our own credibility?

Final Thought

In the end, Nina keeps the baby and names her Bella. Bella is adopted by José and meets her mother in the final scene of the film, when the young girl is five or six. In his quiet way, José has changed the lives of many people. Because he did not judge Nina, she trusted him. Because he listened to Nina, she listened to him. How many times do we hear someone profess a belief or make a statement we find objectionable? Do we listen and respect the other person, or do we talk over her or him, struggling to make our own position heard? José shows us that in some cases, such behaviors can be a matter of life and death.

Cool Runnings

Walt Disney, 1993, Rated A-II and PG

Suggested Use: Conversation Starter

Materials: This film clip requires just your basic setup.

Themes: Sportsmanship, Character, Responsibility

Length of Clip: 02:10

▶ **Begin:** Chapter 18, 1:25:18 Begin as Derice is looking at the pictures when the coach walks in.

■ **End:** 1:27:28 End after the door closes.

Setting the Scene

Based on the story of Jamaica's first Olympic bobsled team, this film provides commentary not just about sports but about what happens in life when we put ourselves first.

Use this scene to talk about cheating in school or in relationships. Challenge the young people to see that all forms of dishonesty are wrong. Invite them to understand that doing something wrong once can lead down that slippery path where other things equally or more wrong become easier to do.

Suggested Process

 Show Clip

Discussion Questions

- Derice wants to know why his coach cheated years ago. Why do you think it was important for Derice to ask the question?

- Have you ever become obsessed with attaining something? What happened when you attained it? Was attaining it as sweet as the desire to pursue it? Why or why not?

- The coach tells Derice, "If you are not enough without gold medals, you'll never be enough with them." What do you think this means for you? Is it possible to seek something for the wrong reasons?

- Think beyond sports for a minute. Can you think of a time when you have been encouraged by others or by your environment to cheat? Why do some people think cheating is okay?

- Do you think young people separate the varying degrees of cheating? For instance, if you cheat once on your homework and get away with it, is it okay to continue cheating? what about cheating on a test? on a girlfriend or boyfriend? At what point do those who think cheating on homework is okay start thinking any kind of cheating is okay?

 # Variation

Consider using this scene as an opportunity to talk about how adults in our community cheat others. Are there politicians in the news that are caught in scandals? What about bankers and others trusted with caring for people's finances? What lessons can be drawn from those situations? Are these people willing to accept responsibility for their actions?

 # Final Thought

In a nonthreatening way, conclude by inviting the young people to discuss why people cheat on homework or tests. Expand the conversation by asking the young people if they think that copying CDs or downloaded music is cheating. Ask them to think about whether you can cheat without actually hurting anyone. Where does the Seventh Commandment ("Thou Shalt Not Steal") fit here?

Entertaining Angels

Paulist Pictures, 1996, Rated A-II and PG-13

SUGGESTED USE: Conversation Starter

MATERIALS: This film clip requires just your basic setup.

THEMES: Social Justice, Reconciliation, Helping the Poor, God's Will for Us, Love

LENGTH OF CLIP: 14:01

> ▶ **Begin:** Chapter 12, 1:30:50 Begin as Dorothy walks down the stairs and is invited to join the meeting.

> ⏹ **End:** 1:44:51 End as Dorothy walks up the stairs to her room, and the scene fades to black.

Setting the Scene

This beautifully told story of Dorothy Day and the beginning of the Catholic Worker movement gives hope to anyone with dreams of changing the world. This scene takes place when Dorothy's coworkers rebel against her desire to take care of the community's most vulnerable. Failing to see that helping those who are poor, those who suffer from alcoholism, those who are mentally ill, and those who are prostitutes is part of their mission, they tell Dorothy, "Enough." They simply want to publish the paper *The Catholic Worker*, which now has more subscribers than they had ever imagined.

Use this scene to discuss how little things can change the world, how getting angry at God can be a natural part of faith development, and how we are called to see Christ in everyone.

Suggested Process

Show Clip

Discussion Questions

- Dorothy's coworkers are tired of caring for those who are poor. They joined the Catholic Worker movement because they "wanted to change the world." Why do you think they believe that helping these people is not a part of that mission? Do you think sometimes people dream so big that they fail to see how the little things really make a difference? Can you think of some examples?

- Dorothy goes to church and screams, "Where are you?" to God. Have you ever wanted to do that? Why? Do you think it is okay to get angry at God? When have you wanted to yell at God? What would you have said during those times in your life?

- Is there some truth to what Dorothy says at church ("you smell, you wet your pants, you vomit . . .")? What effect does that have on people's willingness to help society's most vulnerable?

- Dorothy goes to see her friend Mike, who has a different perspective on her accomplishments. Whom do you depend on for a different perspective on your life?

- Think about Dorothy's reaction to Maggie. What happens that makes her react the way she does? Wouldn't it have been easier to hit Maggie or throw her out? How would you have reacted? What difference do you think it made to Maggie?

- What did you think of the end of this scene? What effect do you think Dorothy's reaction has on her coworkers? Do you think it was hard for Dorothy to admit her mistakes? What do you think Dorothy means when she says, "They are my meeting place with God." Where is your meeting place with God?

 ## Variation

You could split this scene into three parts for some variation on the discussion. First, end the scene after Dorothy leaves the church. Have a discussion about Dorothy's anger with God. Ask the young people if they think it is okay to get angry at God. Second, let the scene play until Dorothy and Mike finish their conversation by the window. Talk about how Dorothy's perspective of the change she has made and Mike's view on reality are very different. Why do we sometimes fail to see the good we do? Third, let the scene play until the end. Talk about Dorothy's comments, "I've been doing a lot of thinking about what God wants me to do with my life," "It begins with these people," and "They are my meeting place with God."

 ## Final Thought

Most of us can relate to Dorothy's rage against God and her plea for God to show up in her life. "I'm not who you thought I was," is Dorothy's great confession to God and is also a stunning indictment of her arrogance. How does she know what God thinks of her? Has God recruited her—or us—because we are somehow better than others? or are we all called to make a difference in the way we live and act? Who do we think we are in God's eyes, and what effect does that have on the way we live?

Evan Almighty

Universal, 2007, Rated A-II and PG

Suggested Use: Prayer

Materials: This film clip requires just your basic setup.

Themes: Prayer, Faith, Relationships, Marriage

Length of Clip: 06:06

> ▶ **Begin:**   Chapter 13, 0:56:12   Begin as Evan pulls into his driveway.
>
> ■ **End:**   1:02:18   End after Joan looks down and sees that her plate is full again.

Setting the Scene

This film is a sequel to *Bruce Almighty*. Evan Baxter is told by God to build an ark, and of course, everyone, including his family, thinks he's crazy. In this scene, Evan's wife, Joan, leaves with the children because Evan's behavior has become so strange. The meat of the clip comes toward the end when God waits on Joan at a restaurant and talks about prayer as an opportunity. One of the prayers God talks about is a prayer that Joan mentioned at the beginning of the movie.

You may show this clip at the beginning of a prayer service and use the questions as a guide to lead the young people in prayerful reflection.

Suggested Process

 Show Clip

Discussion Questions

- Do you know anyone in today's society who people think is crazy for doing the right thing?
- When Evan blames everything on God, saying, "It's not me—it's Him," Joan says that God is ruining their lives. Sometimes we are overwhelmed by God's love in ways that are hard to handle. Have you ever felt like Joan? Do you ever feel like God is asking too much of you? What would your life be like if God loved you less?

 ## Prayer

Invite the young people to gather into a circle. Then give the following directions:

- Recall what God tells Joan about God giving people opportunities instead of direct answers to their prayers. As we go around the circle, share a petition with the group about something for which you would like to pray, and then name the opportunity you think God is giving you in the context of that prayer.

 ## Variation

Take the conversation a little farther with a discussion about God's comment regarding God's wrath. God says that "people love it when God gets angry." Ask the young people if they think that is true. Relate it to the evening news. Ask the following questions:

- Why do people revel in the bad news?
- Why do we count the number of deaths like some sort of sports statistic?

Is what is on the news really news, or is it news because it is the exception to what is really going on in the world? One answer leaves us depressed. The other leaves us faced with a reality that is filled with more hope than sadness. Process this with the young people.

 ## Final Thought

Explain to the participants that earlier in the movie, God tells Evan that to change the world (which was Evan's campaign promise when he ran for Congress), all one needs to do is to start small with one act of random kindess. Encourage the young people to think of an act of random kindness they are called to do each day. Explain that God gives us ample opportunity every day to do what we ought to do—not because we have to, but because we want to.

Field of Dreams

Universal, 1989, Rated A-II and PG

SUGGESTED USE: Conversation Starter

MATERIALS: This film clip requires just your basic setup.

THEMES: Having Faith, Trust, Parent-Child Relationship, Service

LENGTH OF CLIP: 05:51

> ▶ **Begin:** Chapter 32, 1:29:59   Begin as Shoeless Joe jogs off the field to say good-night to Ray.
>
> ◼ **End:**   1:35:50   End as the camera pans across the cornfield.

Setting the Scene

This film stars Kevin Costner as Ray Consella, an Iowa farmer who hears a mysterious voice telling him to turn his cornfield into a baseball diamond. When he does, the mysterious voice gives him more instructions, as the spirits of dead baseball players show up to play on his field. The film reminds us that faith means believing and trusting even when we cannot begin to comprehend the circumstances in our lives. Shoeless Joe Jackson (played by Ray Liotta) was the baseball hero of Ray Consella's father. Shoeless Joe was banned from baseball and became the subject of the last fight Ray had with his father before leaving home. Up to this point in the movie, Ray has done everything the mysterious voice has told him to do: "Build it and he will come," "Go the distance," and "Ease his pain." As Ray realizes he is not invited to go into the cornfield with the ball players—and a friend is—he struggles to understand what these signs mean. He must answer an important question before he can understand anything. It's a question we all must answer.

Suggested Process

 Show Clip

Discussion Questions

- What does this statement mean to you: "Heaven is filled with people who get it."
- Why did Ray want to go into the cornfield with the players? Why was he angry when Shoeless Joe told him he wasn't invited?
- Ray says he has never asked, "What's in it for me?" yet that's exactly what he asks when pressed by Shoeless Joe. Why do you think he built the baseball diamond and followed the instructions of the mysterious voice? What motivates you to serve?
- What was the question Ray had to answer before he began to understand the meaning of his experience?
- Do you think Ray's father was already present, or do you think he appeared just for this scene? If you watch the entire film, you'll see that he was visible the whole time. Even when he recognized his father, Ray still didn't completely understand. What did Shoeless Joe's comments reveal about Ray's experience of faith?

 ## Variation

Stop the film after Ray responds to Shoeless Joe, "I'm asking, what's in it for me?" and discuss the purpose of community service. Ask the young people what motivates them to serve—the necessity of service hours for school or church? because our parents require it? something else?

 ## Final Thought

It is only when Ray begins to understand that the experience of building the baseball diamond was rooted in faith that he is able to recognize his father. Ask the young people:

- What do we need to understand, or "get," in order to finally recognize our Father?

Gandhi

Columbia Pictures, 1982, Rated A-II and PG

SUGGESTED USE: Conversation Starter

MATERIALS: This film clip requires just your basic setup.

THEMES: Social Justice, Courage, Nonviolence, Character, Vocation

LENGTH OF CLIP: 09:30

> ▶ **Begin:** Chapter 17, 2:01:34   Begin as Gandhi sits alone on the wall near the water.
>
> ⏹ **End:**   2:11:04   End as the newsreel ends.

Setting the Scene

It would take several sessions to unpack all the great scenes in this film and to help young people digest the film's message for our time. This scene, Gandhi's march to the ocean to make salt, is as powerful as any other. Fighting for independence from Great Britain, Gandhi leads the fight without raising a hand. Though not the first to promote nonviolence, Gandhi uses a method that is certainly the most celebrated in our modern history.

Use this scene to discuss the arrogance of the British government, specifically those charged with overseeing Britain's local control of India, and the power of one man willing to risk arrest—even death—to do what he knows he must.

Suggested Process

 Show Clip

Discussion Questions

- Gandhi says he can remember singing this as a young boy: "A true disciple knows another's woes as his own. He bows to all and despises none." What do you think that means? What does that challenge you to do? Have you heard that message proclaimed another way?

- Gandhi says that when he was a boy, the priest acted as though it did not matter which book was being read, so long as God was being worshiped. Why is that so difficult in parts of the world? Why can religion be such a force of controversy?

- Why do the government officials choose to ignore Gandhi's march to the sea? Why is it important for the government to control the salt? How do governments use food and water to control people in the world today?

- Action against a government often results in violence. Why do you think the people are so willing and eager to follow Gandhi? What do you think he means when he says: "They are not in control. We are." Is he right?

- At the sea, Gandhi tells the Indian people to claim the salt as their own. The news media portrays him as challenging the might of the British Empire. How can something as simple as salt be such a powerful weapon in Gandhi's fight for India's independence?

 ## Variation

Extend the session by playing the next several minutes of the film. Talk about the reaction of the British leaders. What effect has Gandhi had on their government? Continue playing until the soldiers stop the selling of salt and the people remind one another not to fight back. Ask the young people the following questions:

- Could you be so passive in the face of such tyranny?

- When are you called to be like Gandhi and make a change in society?

- What are the ills around you that you could seek to challenge in nonviolent ways?

 ## Final Thought

The quotation most often attributed to Gandhi is his appeal "Be the change you wish to see in the world." Use that powerful mantra to talk about the change the young people could bring to their families, their parishes, their schools, or their communities. Is it possible for young people to be elements of change?

Goal: The Dream Begins

Touchstone Pictures, 2006, Rated A-II and PG-13

SUGGESTED USE: Prayer

MATERIALS: This film clip requires just your basic setup.

THEMES: Parent-Child Relationship, Self-Worth, Reconciliation, Responsibility

LENGTH OF CLIP: 04:25

▶ **Begin:** Chapter 17, 1:33:41   Begin as Santi talks on the phone.

⏹ **End:**   1:38:06   End after Santi kicks the ball.

Setting the Scene

Brought to the United States from Mexico as a boy, Santiago Munez has one dream—to play soccer with a professional team. To do so he must overcome his own demons, including a relationship with his father that, though miles away, affected his frame of mind. In this scene, Santi learns of his father's death and, like any good son, heads to the airport to return home. Soon, however, he is back at practice telling the coach why he did not get on the plane.

Use this scene to talk about how some relationships give us strength while others leave us wanting more. Also discuss who has power over us, who influences us, and about whose opinion we care about.

Suggested Process

 Show Clip

Discussion Questions

- Santi's relationship with his father is not a good one, so why do you think he cries when he hears the news that his father is dead?

- It was Santi's father who brought him to America and opened the door to the possibilities for him. What opportunities have your parents created for you? What opportunities exist simply because of your place of birth?

- When do we see young people allowing others to make them feel worthless? Is it possible for others to take away our aspirations? How? Why do you think young people give away their power?

- Who is your "boss"? For Santi it was his coach, who could make him feel unimportant, and only then if Santi listened. Who has that power in your life? Why?

- In this scene, one of the other players takes responsibility for his actions. The coach tells him that the others are looking to him as an example. Who looks to you for direction?

 Prayer

Conclude with a prayer for immigrants, undocumented workers, and those whose dreams require them to seek a new life in a strange world.

 Variation

Use this scene, and film, to talk about the plight of immigrants in the United States. Ask the young people the following questions:

- Are undocumented persons a problem to be solved or an opportunity for ministry? Why?

- Why do some people react so passionately about immigration?

- What effect do immigrants have on your community?

Challenge the young people to do some research about the plight of immigrants in their community. If possible, arrange for the young people to gather with young people from a different cultural ministry and share their stories of opportunities.

 Final Thought

This film is about identifying dreams and working hard to achieve them. More than that, it is about the power we give to other people when we allow them to tell us whether we are good enough, strong enough, or worth the trouble at all. Why we give this power away is a mystery. Challenge the young people to take back the power, to think of themselves as strong enough to do anything they can imagine. Remind them that we are loved unconditionally by God, and perfect in God's eyes. We are forgiven. We are a dream fulfilled.

I Am David

Artisan Films, 2003, Rated A-II and PG

SUGGESTED USE: Activity, Prayer

MATERIALS: This film clip requires just your basic setup, plus a Bible.

THEMES: Self-Sacrifice, Trust, Friendship, Redemption

LENGTH OF CLIP: 07:48

▶	**Begin:**	Chapter 14, 1:15:07	Begin as Sophie comes down the stairs.
■	**End:**	1:22:55	End as David walks into the bookstore.

Setting the Scene

Based on Anne Holm's bestselling book *North to Freedom* (Harcourt Brace & Company and Methuen & Company, 1965), this film follows young David as he escapes from the communist Belene Prison Camp in Bulgaria during the war and tries to find his mother.

This particular scene is a great introduction to a prayer service about friendship and self-sacrifice. Challenge the young people to listen to the reading and then pray for their friends by name.

Suggested Process

 Show Clip

Discussion Questions

- David asks why most people do bad things. Is his assertion that most people do bad things accurate? How would you answer his question?

- David had been imprisoned in a communist concentration camp during the Bulgarian war and escaped after several years. This makes it very difficult for him to trust people. Have you ever been afraid to trust people? Why?

- Sophie tells David that he will learn, in time, how to trust people. How do you know when you can trust someone?

- Always frightened by the police and guards, David is finally able to say hello to the policeman he encounters in the church. Why do you think this is so? Do you think Sophie's wisdom had anything to do with it?

- In a flashback scene, we learn that David stole a piece of soap while he was in the communist concentration camp. Knowing that David would die for doing this, his friend Johannes takes the soap from David and gives his own life for David. Why do you think remembering this and listening to the music finally brings a smile to David's face?

 Activity

Read aloud Sirach 6:5–17 and give the young people a few moments to reflect on the passage. Then ask the following questions:

- How many qualities of friendship can you name?

- Who are the "faithful shelters" in your life?

 Variation

Use this scene and the discussion questions—including the Scripture reading—with the young people. Gather the young people in a circle and ask them to name a person who is their faithful friend or sturdy shelter. Then go around the circle a second time and challenge the young people to identify ways that person provides shelter for them in their times of need.

 Final Thought

What better challenge to us as followers of Christ than to provide safe shelter to one another. What a treasure it can be to find someone you trust and love as the reading indicates. Ask the young people to think about who those people are in their lives.

Invincible

SUGGESTED USE: Conversation Starter

MATERIALS: This film clip requires just your basic setup.

THEMES: Character, Sportsmanship, Reaching Our Dreams, Friendship, Self-Respect

LENGTH OF CLIP: 03:52

▶ **Begin:** Chapter 12, 1:03:28   Begin as the coaches are sitting around the table.

■ **End:** 1:07:20   End when the coach says, "Welcome to the Eagles."

Setting the Scene

The story of Vince Papale is a story of heart and character. When the new coach in working-class Philadelphia has open tryouts for the local professional team, Vince gives it a shot. In this scene, we see the coach's willingness to take a chance on Vince, even if no other coach agrees with him. Even Vince's teammates want him to be cut from the team.

Use this scene to challenge the young people to find out what makes up the coach's mind and to discuss whether sports—and other challenges we face—build character or reveal it.

Suggested Process

 Show Clip

Discussion Questions

- Though it would never happen nowadays, why was having open tryouts for a professional football team a good idea? What does it teach us about how we might approach a difficult problem?

- One of the coaches tells Dick Vermeil: "People don't want heart. . . . They want wins." Do you think this is true? Why? How do you see the pressures of professional sports trickling down to the your middle school or high school?

- Why do you think Vince's teammates want him cut from the team? What do you think finally makes up the coach's mind?

- Talk about what Carol Vermeil says to her husband about character. Can you think of a situation where you have been "up against it" and your character has been revealed?

- Why do you think Coach Vermeil was so surprised when Vince asked how he was doing? Do you think that had any influence on the coach's decision?

 # Variation

Extend the session by letting the scene play for another minute or two. Let the young people see how Vince's friends react. Even though some are out on strike and money is tight, they rejoice at the success of their friend. Joe, in particular, says, "I'm good now," indicating that the news of Vince's making the team has changed his perspective. Ask the young people:

- What does this scene say about the power of friendship?

- What does it say about the qualities we should seek in those we are close to?

 # Final Thought

To conclude tell the young people that Vince Papale scored a game-winning touchdown in the second game of the season (September 1976) after a dismal showing in the first game and was finally accepted by his teammates. He played three seasons with the Eagles. Coach Dick Vermeil led the Eagles to a Super Bowl win in 1981.

Lars and the Real Girl

MGM/Sidney Kimmel, 2007, Rated A-II and PG-13

SUGGESTED USE: Conversation Starter

MATERIALS: This film clip requires just your basic setup.

THEMES: Acceptance, Judgment, Relationships

LENGTH OF CLIP: 02:38

> ▶ **Begin:** Chapter 9, 0:37:10   Begin as the church members sit in a circle discussing Lars and Bianca.

> ◼ **End:** 0:39:48   End when Bianca and Lars walk away from the church.

Setting the Scene

This film is number six on the USCCB's list of top-ten films for 2007 (tied with *Juno*). Lars has a difficult time relating to people. He keeps to himself, avoiding human touch and most conversations. Then one day he orders a doll on the Internet and everything changes. Bianca, the doll, brings Lars to life, but how will the small town react to a grown man dating a doll?

Use this scene, where Lars's brother and sister-in-law enlist the help of other church members to accept Bianca, to discuss acceptance of those who are different. Bianca certainly is one of a kind.

Suggested Process

 Show Clip

Discussion Questions

- What do you think about the reactions of the church members? How would you react? How do Mrs. Gruner's comments change everything? What do you think she means when she says that "we all have our things."

- The priest welcomes Bianca, and Mrs. Gruner offers Bianca flowers. Others stare and whisper. One child even runs after Bianca, presumably to see her up close. Do you think this reaction is normal? Why do some people have a hard time accepting those who are different?

- Have you ever known someone who reached out to another person who was having trouble fitting in? What did that person do to reach out to another?

- How does our society deal with mental illness? Do we, as a whole, do a good job welcoming those who are different? What would happen if we were treated like those we laugh at or scorn? How would that make us feel?

 Variation

Let the scene play for a few more minutes to see how Lars interacts with Bianca. He treats her like she is real because to him, she is. In time the rest of the community begins to treat her as a member of their community as well. Bianca gets a job, she gets a haircut, and she volunteers at the hospital. Ask the young people the following questions:

- What do you think will happen to Lars when everyone else starts treating Bianca as one of their own?

- What does it say about Lars that people are so willing to welcome Bianca?

 Final Thought

Discuss the following questions with the young people:

- Why do we sometimes react so negatively to people who are different?

- Why does society seem to have such a rigid definition of what (or who) is normal versus abnormal? But who is to say what is right, and who is to say that Lars's relationship with Bianca is wrong?

In loving Bianca, Lars learns to love others. By accepting Bianca with open arms, the community shows how much they love Lars. A little acceptance goes a long way and changes Lars's life. From Bianca he learns how to love and be loved. From the community, he slowly learns that he is the only one who needs convincing that he has always been accepted and loved.

Madagascar

DreamWorks SKG, 2005, Rated A-II and PG

SUGGESTED USE: Activity

MATERIALS: This film clip requires just your basic setup, plus an index card and a pen or pencil for each young person.

THEMES: Happiness, Contentment, Friendship

LENGTH OF CLIP: 04:55

▶ **Begin:** Chapter 3, 0:08:36   Begin as the zookeepers push the meal trays through the zoo.

⏹ **End:** 0:13:31   End when Marty sits down along the wall but before Alex starts to sing.

Setting the Scene

Marty, Alex, Gloria, and Melmen are animals in the Central Park Zoo. Entertaining the crowds and being waited on by zoo staff is an easy life. But it is not enough for Marty. He longs to be in the wild, running free and out from behind bars. In this scene, he makes such a wish when his friends throw him a birthday party. Thinking his wish silly, they mock him for wanting to leave the zoo. Unhappy with his present state in life and now feeling dejected, Marty returns to his pen.

Use this scene to introduce the activity and to discuss why some people are content in their current state while others always seem to want more.

Suggested Process

Show Clip

Discussion Questions

- Everything seems to be provided for the animals. They have food, they are well groomed, and they have one another. Still Marty is not happy. Why do you think he wishes for more?
- Why do Marty's friends think his idea is dumb? Do you think his demands are unreasonable? Is it wrong to want more than you have?
- Gloria tells Alex to give Marty a pep talk. Whom do you depend upon to help you feel better when you are unhappy with your current situation in life?
- What does it mean to be happy? What does it take? For some of the animals, happiness is inside the zoo. For Marty happiness is a dream outside the zoo's walls. What is happiness for you?

 Activity

Distribute the index cards, and pens or pencils to the young people and share the following directions:

- Using your index card, write your recipe for happiness. Think about what is required to make you happy. List at least five ingredients that are necessary to make you happy.

When the participants have completed the task, ask the following questions:

- Do you have all of the ingredients on your list? If not, what do you need to do to get some of them?

 Variation

After the young people finish writing their recipes, have a conversation about happiness versus contentment. Ask the following questions:

- What is the difference between happiness and contentment?
- Can we be content and still be unhappy?

Help the young people unpack what Jesus says is required for happiness. Look at Matthew 5:1–12 and Luke 6:20–26 as well as the parable of the rich young fool, in Luke 12:16–21. Ask the following questions:

- Do any of your recipes include service to others or to God? If not, why not?
- Does helping others make you happy? Does serving God make you happy? If so, add some extra ingredients to your recipes.

 Final Thought

Ask the young people to think about the following questions:

- What is the difference between hope, contentment, and happiness?
- Does *hope* imply that we must be committed to change?
- Can contentment lead to being in a rut?
- Can happiness be improved upon?
- Is it possible, if we are happy, to become more happy?

Millions

SUGGESTED USE: Activity

MATERIALS: This film clip requires just your basic setup, plus a sheet of newsprint and a marker for each small group of four or five and a roll of tape to hang the newsprint. For the session variation, each young person will need a Bible.

THEMES: Generosity, Responsibility, Accountability, Sacrifice

LENGTH OF CLIP: 03:53

> ▶ **Begin:** Chapter 12, 0:45:23 Begin as Damian fills the envelopes with money.
>
> ⏹ **End:** 0:49:16 End as the scene changes.

Setting the Scene

Damian finds a bag filled with money—or rather the bag finds him. The money, in British pounds, will be worthless once the United Kingdom switches to euros, leaving Damian only a short time to give the money away. A faithful child with an active imagination, Damian is often visited by saints who give him advice on how to spend the money or how to get along with his family now that his mother has died. In this scene, Saint Peter visits and tells his version of what happened at the miracle of loaves and fishes.

Use this clip to introduce the activity, which challenges the young people to see what they can accomplish with the gifts they have at their disposal.

Suggested Process

 Show Clip

Discussion Questions

- Damian wants to do good things with the money but asks Saint Peter if that is still possible, now that he knows the money is stolen. How would you answer the question? Can something good come out of a sinful situation?

- Saint Peter tells Damian about what "really" happened at the miracle of the loaves and fishes. Which would have been a greater miracle—feeding five thousand or getting everybody to share what they already had?

- Why does Saint Peter think that getting everyone to share was one of Jesus's best miracles? What do you think he means when he says that after the boy stood up, everyone there "just got bigger"?

- How is Saint Peter's story applicable today? Are resources shared fairly in today's society? Do you think it is possible to change that? How?

 Activity

Gather the young people into small groups of four or five and distribute a sheet of newsprint and a marker to each small group. Share with them the following directions:

- Make a list of the resources and gifts each one of you brings to the group. Then discuss what you can accomplish if you share those resources. Think big. What is possible if you share what you have in your possession right now?

 Variations

In the clip, Saint Peter says that sometimes miracles come from something that is "dead simple." Have the young people choose one of the following miracles from the Scriptures: the miraculous catch of fish (Luke 5:4–11), the miracle of the ten lepers (Luke 17:11–19), the miracle of the water made into wine (John 2:1–11), the miracle of the blind man at Bethsaida (Mark 8:22–26), Lazarus raised from the dead (John 11:38–44), Peter and the healing of the paralytic (Acts of the Apostles 9:32–35), or the healing of the Centurion's servant (Matthew 8:5–13 and Luke 7:1–10). Instruct them to read the Scripture passage and then retell the miracle in the same way as Saint Peter. They may work individually or in small groups. Challenge them to come up with a more simple explanation. Invite them to share their stories with the large group.

If you want this activity to be more effective, use this clip during Lent and follow your discussion with lunch. Give some young people bag lunches with lots of food and give others bag lunches with very little. Then see what happens. Have a discussion with the young people after they have finished their lunch. Ask them the following questions:

- Did anyone have food left over from lunch?

- Did anyone share some of their lunch with someone who had less food ? Why or why not?

- Is anyone still hungry?

 Final Thought

A fantastic take on Jesus's feeding of five thousand, this scene encourages generosity and imagination. Think beyond the film for a minute and see what the young people have to say about ways our society could share resources to improve the lives of others. This take on the miracle illustrates what Christianity is all about: community. Christian tradition tells us that unless we take care of one another, unless we love one another and fogive one another, we will all suffer.

National Treasure: Book of Secrets

Walt Disney, 2007, Rated A-II and PG

SUGGESTED USE: Conversation Starter

MATERIALS: This film clip requires just your basic setup.

THEMES: Sacrifice, Service, Moral Decision Making, Reconciliation

LENGTH OF CLIP: 12:41

▶ **Begin:** Chapter 16, 1:40:06   Begin as Ben and the crew enter the room filled with water.

⏹ **End:** 1:52:47   End as the group sees the light at the end of the tunnel and begins to follow it.

Setting the Scene

This sequel does a nice job of following up on the first *National Treasure* (Walt Disney, 2004, rated A-II and PG). In the first movie, Ben Gates's family name has been smeared by a renegade treasure hunter. As a result, Ben, his girlfriend, Abigail, and his partner from the first movie, Riley, are forced, along with Ben's parents, to search for the City of Gold in the mountains of South Dakota. In this scene, they discover El Dorado and also quickly discover that there is only one way out. For the majority to survive, one person must stay behind and hold the door open for the others, even if it means sacrificing his or her life in the process. Ben offers to stay, over the objections of everyone except Mitch.

Use this scene to talk about self-sacrifice, service to others, and our willingness (or not) to do both.

Suggested Process

Show Clip

Discussion Questions

- Ben and his family have been forced to hunt for treasure by Mitch Wilkinson, who smeared the family name of Ben and his father in order to enlist their help. For Mitch it is all about making a name for his own family and leaving his family's mark on history.

- As soon as Ben and Mitch get the door open and Mitch sees a way to escape, he lets the door shut, blocking the way. Do you know people like Mitch, who are concerned about their own interests only rather than the interests of others? Throughout history what have such people taught us?

- Why do you think Ben is willing to stay behind when clearly he has the most to lose? Do you think Ben would have offered to stay even if Mitch had not wielded a knife?

- Even when the tables turn and Ben is able to get out, he offers to help Mitch, who put them all in danger in the first place. What obligations do we have to people who are mean to us?

- Why is Mitch so eager to get credit for the discovery? Why is having fame or fortune so important to some people?

 ## Variation

Ask the young people the following questions:

- Does Mitch's willingness to stay undo the evil he has done in endangering the lives of the others?

- Is he willing to stay to save the others because there really is no other option?

Talk to the young people about those who put us in danger, whose own selfishness risks their souls and lives, as well as ours. Ask these questions:

- Do we have an obligation to try to save them, or should we let them destroy themselves?

- What if it is not a tunnel filled with water we are trying to get out of? Think beyond this scene. Are we obliged to help those who are addicted to drugs or alcohol? What about those—like Mitch—who are addicted to power? What should our lives teach them?

 ## Final Thought

Jesus sacrificed himself willingly. He knew that no one could be reconciled to the Father if he did not say yes to death on the cross. Use the following questions to start a discussion with the young people:

- What are we willing to do to make similar, smaller sacrifices in our lives? Are we willing to risk our reputation to help those in our schools and communities who are unloved? Are we willing to risk our time, talent, and treasure to volunteer for a cause? Are we willing to risk anything for anyone?

Challenge the young people to make a list of things they are willing to sacrifice in service to others.

Raising Helen

SUGGESTED USE: Conversation Starter

MATERIALS: This film clip requires just your basic setup. For the session variation, gather also a sheet of newsprint and a marker for each small group of four or five.

THEMES: Death, Suffering, Dreams, Relationships

LENGTH OF CLIP: 02:34

> ▶ **Begin:** Chapter 10, 1:24:47   Begin as soon as the scene changes to basketball practice.
>
> ⏹ **End:** 1:27:21   End after Henry makes a basket.

Setting the Scene

Helen's sister and brother-in-law are killed in a car accident and Helen, a New Yorker living the high life, inherits their three children. Now suddenly a parent, Helen has a lot of growing up to do. This scene, after Helen seems to be getting things together, shows Helen dealing with Henry and his sudden lack of interest in a sport he and his father both once loved.

Use this scene to talk to the young people about death, about the change sudden loss can bring, and about how (as the funeral liturgy tells us) life is changed, not ended. Because this scene can evoke memories of loss, be careful how you use it. Know your audience.

Suggested Process

 Show Clip

Discussion Questions

- Henry clearly isn't trying his best. Why? How long do you think it's okay to mourn a loss? Is the answer the same for everyone?

- Why doesn't Henry want to smile? Do you think people who have experienced a sudden loss behave that way? Why?

- The preface to the Eucharistic prayer, which we say when we celebrate a funeral in the Catholic Church, states, "Lord, for your faithful people life is changed, not ended." What do you think this means? Does it mean, as Henry believes, that people who die are watching us from heaven, or is there more to it than that?

- Helen tells Henry that the only thing sadder than his parents not being here is Henry's not doing what he loves. Do you think that's true? Have you ever stopped doing what you love when you lost someone? Why?

- How do we make sure that those we have lost are remembered? How can our lives be a testament to what they have taught us?

 ## Variation

For an optional activity, ask the young people to form small groups of four or five and have each person name someone close to them who has died. If some of the young people have not experienced such a loss, they can name anyone (even someone famous). Ask the young people to share the names of the people they chose with the large group. As they do so, write the names on the newsprint. Then invite the young people to come up with at least one way they can honor these lives with their own. Record the answers next to the corresponding names on the newsprint.

 ## Final Thought

Ask the young people how our actions, outside of Sunday Mass, commemorate that Jesus once walked on earth as a human being.

Remember the Titans

Buena Vista, 2002, Rated A-II and PG

SUGGESTED USE: Conversation Starter

MATERIALS: This film clip requires just your basic setup.

THEMES: Leadership, Sportsmanship, Character, Race Relations, Teamwork

LENGTH OF CLIP: 01:39

> ▶ **Begin:** Chapter 9, 0:29:09 — Begin as Bertier and Big Ju come around the corner and start talking.

> ⬛ **End:** 0:30:48 — End with the statement "Attitude reflects leadership, Captain."

Setting the Scene

This film is a great modern football movie. Telling the story of a 1971 community torn apart by mistrust and hatred, the movie depicts the struggle of a town whose members pulled together by their sons and their team.

This scene provides a great opportunity to use a sports metaphor with young people who may not play sports. It shows how two young people who do not trust each other must figure out a way to work together if the team is to ever become a team.

Suggested Process

 Show Clip

Discussion Questions

- Whose attitude is worse—the player who believes there is no team or the player who believes his teammate is a waste of God-given talent?

- When someone is given a task, or accepts a position on a team, what responsibility does that person have to give his or her best effort? If this is true for a team, is it also true for a group project at school or church?

- What if you do not like the people you are assigned to work on a project with? What effect can that have on the project? on the attitudes of the workers? What is your responsibility to do your best in this kind of situation?

- What do you think of the statement "Attitude reflects leadership, Captain." Is that true? Is it fair? Even if the leader is a poor one, do we still have a responsibility to approach our work with the right attitude? Why is that so hard?

- When has your attitude affected the work of a team or group? How did it affect the work?

 Variation

Think beyond sports. Use this scene with a group of young people getting ready to head out on a service trip to talk about the attitude they will need to have while accomplishing this work. Have the young people consider how a leader's attitude affects the experience. Ask the following questions:

- What if a leader has a negative attitude?

- What if the attitudes of the workers are poor?

- What will the work look like at the end of the week if the attitudes and leadership are negative?

 Final Thought

Ask the young people these questions:

- When you look at another person, what do you see?

- Is race a part of what you see? height? weight? gender?

- How can we see someone for who she or he really is without letting our own blindness or bigotry get in the way?

Rudy

TriStar Pictures, 1993, Rated A-II and PG

SUGGESTED USE: Activity

MATERIALS: This film clip requires just your basic setup, plus an index card and a pen or pencil for each young person.

THEME: Dreams, Expectations, Parent-Child Relationships

LENGTH OF CLIP: 03:08

▶ **Begin:** Chapter 7, 0:21:22 Begin as Rudy sits on the bench and his father approaches.

⏹ **End:** 0:24:30 End as the bus pulls away and Rudy looks out the window.

Setting the Scene

Rudy is a great film about chasing your dreams. In this scene, Rudy has decided to chase his dream and leave for Notre Dame. Much to his surprise, his dad shows up at the bus station and tries to talk him out of it.

Use this scene to introduce the session activity.

Suggested Process

 Show Clip

Discussion Questions

- Rudy's dad says his son is "chasing a stupid dream." Do you think that is a fair description from the father's perspective?

- Do you think your parents do a good job expressing that they want only what is best for you? What advice would you give them to help them improve?

- Have your parents ever compared you to one of your siblings? How did that make you feel? How do you think it made your brother or sister feel?

- Is a dream the same thing as a goal? If not, what do you think is the difference?

 ## Activity

Distribute an index card and a pen or pencil to each young person. Then offer the following directions:

- Using the index card you have been given, write down three to five dreams you have for your future.

- Next to each write down what you need to do to make that dream come true.

- Finally, add the names of those people in your life you can depend on for encouragement as you follow those dreams.

 ## Final Thought

Ask the young people the following questions:

- Do you think it is difficult for parents with multiple children to avoid comparing one child to another?

- What advice would you give parents who struggle with this dilemma?

Shadowlands

HBO Films, 1993, Rated A-II and PG

SUGGESTED USE: Prayer

MATERIALS: This film clip requires just your basic setup.

THEMES: Prayer, Accepting God's Will

LENGTH OF CLIP: 00:35

> ▶ **Begin:**   Chapter 16, 1:29:46   Begin as Jack enters the vesting area.
>
> ◼ **End:**   1:30:21   End as Jack walks away.

Setting the Scene

Retelling the story of C. S. Lewis, whose nickname is Jack, and his love affair with an American divorcée, this clip comes at a time when Joy seems to be rallying from her cancer. Jack's friends ask how she is and then comment on how hard Jack has been praying. "Now God is answering your prayer," his friend says. In Jack's 30-second response to his friend, we hear the true definition of what prayer is meant to be in our lives and in our relationship with God.

Use this scene and the questions that follow as a way to introduce the closing prayer, or as an opening prayer for a conversation about listening to God.

Suggested Process

   Show Clip

Discussion Questions

- What are the reasons Jack gives for why he prays? In what ways do they mirror your own reasons for prayer?

- How has prayer changed you? Can you think of a specific example in which your attitude, faith, or circumstance was changed by prayer?

 ## Prayer

Conclude with a prayer for intercessions, asking the young people, "For what shall we pray today?"

 ## Variation

Ask the young people to think about some great leaders in their lives or in history. Guide them to think about people who clearly have or have had a close relationship with God (Gandhi, Mother Teresa, Pope John Paul II, Jesus). Ask the following questions:

- How did these leaders' intense prayer change them?

- How was their prayer more of a conversation with God than a list of demands?

- Why were others so eager to follow them?

- What was it that they had that others wanted?

- Is the answer wrapped up somehow in the way that prayer was a call to conversion for them to change or improve? What about Jack's comment that he "can't help himself . . . waking and sleeping"? What does it take to have a prayer life like that?

 ## Final Thought

We have all seen the stickers that say "Prayer Changes People," but this clip provides a real example of how that can happen. One of the hardest lessons we need to learn is to connect the idea of God's will with our own. Jack's friends assume he is praying for Joy to get well, when in fact, Jack is finally—through prayer—coming to realize how much he loves Joy and how he must accept her suffering as part of their relationship. Prayer makes him a better husband, a better friend, and eventually, a good father.

Think about a time God spoke to you through prayer and you were changed. If you feel comfortable, share that experience with the young people.

Shrek the Third

DreamWorks, 2007, Rated A-II and PG

Suggested Use: Conversation Starter

Materials: This film clip requires just your basic setup.

Themes: Self-Esteem, Self-Image, Self-Worth

Length of Clip: 08:22

▶ **Begin:** Chapter 16, 1:10:23 Begin as the curtain parts.

■ **End:** 1:18:45 End when Arthur accepts the crown.

Setting the Scene

Prince Charming is in love—mostly with himself. Still jealous that Shrek won Fiona's heart, and the kingdom, he seeks to destroy Shrek. Young Arthur is the rightful heir to the throne but has always been told he is a loser. When you hear negative feedback often enough, you begin to believe it, as Arthur has. In this scene, he finally realizes he is the only one whose opinion counts and so decides to take a risk in saving Shrek.

Use this scene to talk about self-esteem, self-respect, and self-worth.

Suggested Process

 Show Clip

Discussion Questions

- Why do you think some people believe violence is the only way to solve a problem?

- If you have always been told you are worthless or a loser, which is easier to believe: that you are what people say you are, or that you are worth much more than others say? Why?

- Do you believe people can change? If people are evil, can they become good? If people are good, can circumstances make them evil?

- Arthur says that just because people treat you like a loser does not mean that you are one. What does he mean when he says that sometimes we are the only ones standing in our way?

 Variation

Pause the film at the scene when Shrek is stabbed (and before he smiles) and have a conversation about sacrifice. Why does Shrek jump in front of the sword? Then continue the scene until Arthur takes the crown.

 Final Thought

Words can be powerful. Ask the young people to think of a time when the words of another had such a powerful impact on them that they can still remember the words verbatim.

Superman Returns

Warner Brothers, 2006, Rated A-II and PG-13

SUGGESTED USE: Conversation Starter

MATERIALS: This film clip requires just your basic setup.

THEMES: God's Presence in the World, Prayer, Despair

LENGTH OF CLIP: 06:20

▶ **Begin:** Chapter 19, 1:08:40 Begin as Lois walks away from Clark and gets into the elevator.

⬛ **End:** 1:15:00 End as Lois and Superman fly across the top of the water.

Setting the Scene

This wonderful installment of the Superman series brings Superman back to his adopted nation after a five-year absence. During Superman's absence Lois Lane, angry that Superman abandoned the world, wrote a Pulitzer Prize–winning article called "Why the World Doesn't Need Superman." This scene has Superman confronting Lois about the article and gives us his perspective on why the world does, in fact, need a savior.

Suggested Process

 Show Clip

Discussion Questions

- Lois is angry that Superman left. So angry, in fact, that she wrote a Pulitzer Prize–winning article, "Why the World Doesn't Need Superman." In her conversation with the caped crusader, she expresses this anger and asks, "How could you leave us like that?" Have you ever felt abandoned by those you love? What did you do to get over it?

- Lois says, "The world doesn't need a savior . . . and neither do I." What signs exist in our world today that lead you to believe that some people think Lois's statement is true? Can you think of signs in our world that prove the statement false?

- Lois agrees to go "up" with Superman, and as they fly, he asks her what she hears. "Nothing," she replies. What do you think about Superman's response?

- "I hear everything," Superman says. Do you think God hears everything? What does this say about how we could or should pray?

- Superman tells Lois, "You wrote that the world doesn't need a savior, but every day I hear people crying for one." How do people cry out for a savior in today's world? How do you?

 Variation

Use Lois's comments about Superman leaving ("Clark said you left without saying good-bye because it was too unbearable.") as a jumping-off point for a conversation about the good-byes in our lives. Have the young people recall a time when someone left without saying good-bye. Ask the following questions:

- What did it feel like?

- Why do we feel abandoned and lonely when that happens?

- How can these experiences leave us bitter?

 Final Thought

In those moments of our lives when we feel abandoned, we can act out, as Lois did, and become bitter (which explains why she wrote the article), turning away from the savior. Or we can cry out to that savior we feel has abandoned us and seek peace. One reaction leaves us empty, the other, perhaps, in time, fulfilled.

The Incredibles

Walt Disney, 2004, Rated A-II and PG

SUGGESTED USE: Activity

MATERIALS: This film clip requires just your basic setup, plus a sheet of paper and a pen or pencil for each participant.

THEMES: Family, Courage, Giftedness, Vocation

LENGTH OF CLIP: 04:46

> ▶ **Begin:**   Chapter 18, 1:10:50   Begin as the family is screaming in the water.
>
> ⏹ **End:**   1:15:36   End after Violet puts on her mask.

Setting the Scene

Have you ever wanted to be a superhero? This film, about undercover superheroes who come out of retirement to save the world, provides some great discussion about self-discovery, family dynamics, and more.

Use this scene to talk about what kind of superhero the young people would choose to become and what their powers would bring to the world. Would they use their powers for good, or would they use them to get what they want for themselves?

Suggested Process

 Show Clip

Discussion Questions

- If you could be a superhero or, more spefically, have a superpower, what would that power look like? Can you think of any specific situations you could have changed if you had had that power?

- In this scene, Mr. Incredible thinks he has lost everything. He does not know his family escaped the rockets, and yet he still refuses to kill. Why? Why do some people turn to violence while others do not?

- Elastigirl asks her kids to trust her. Why is it important to trust your parents? Have you ever struggled with trusting them? Why?

- Though you may not be a superhero, is it true that "you have more power than you realize"? Do your parents ever ask too much of you?

- Do you believe it is true that evil powers are at work in the world? What can you do, with the power you have been given, to stop it?

 Activity

Distribute a sheet of paper and a pen or pencil to each young person and then offer the following directions:

- Imagine that you have superpowers. Write a news article from a third-party perspective about how you have used your superpowers. Imagine yourself in a hero's role. Do you wear a costume? If so, what does it look like? Would you pass your powers on to your children? What, if anything, would render you powerless?

 Final Thought

Share this final thought with the teens. Even faced with the thought of having nothing, Mr. Incredible chooses life. In a later scene, one of the characters says that choosing life is not a sign of weakness and that choosing to end it is not a sign of power. Ask the young people the following question:

- How can you, with your newfound superpowers, bring new life to a broken world?

The Mighty Ducks

Walt Disney, 1992, Rated A-II and PG

SUGGESTED USE: Conversation Starter

MATERIALS: This film clip requires just your basic setup.

THEME: Fair Play, Sportsmanship, Teamwork, Coaching

LENGTH OF CLIP: 02:57

▶ **Begin:**   Chapter 7, 0:28:22   Begin as Coach Bombay, standing on the ice, teaches the players how to cheat.

■ **End:**   0:31:19   End when the players start walking out of the locker room in disgust.

Setting the Scene

This is a great movie about sportsmanship and teamwork. This movie proves that it is never too late to learn what fair play is all about.

Use this clip with athletes as you prepare for a new season or to have a conversation about sportsmanship and the qualities of a good coach.

Suggested Process

 Show Clip

Discussion Questions

- Coach Bombay takes the job of coaching this team because he is ordered to do so by a judge. Why do you think he resorts to cheating instead of trying to teach these players the skills they need to learn? What makes a good coach?

- Has anyone ever asked you to cheat? Have you ever known someone who cheated and got caught? What are the ramifications of cheating?

- Charlie tells Coach Bombay, "You can't make me cheat." Is this true? Isn't the coach in charge of the team? Don't players have to do what he or she says?

- Who are the other victims here? Think about what the dad says when he comes to take his kids from the locker room. How has he been cheated?

- Why do you think people are so disappointed when professional athletes cheat? Is it fair that we tend to hold them to a higher standard?

 ## Variation

This would be a great clip to use with coaches to introduce the topic of fair play or to show that it is not just the young people who are cheated when a coach does a poor job.

 ## Final Thought

Ask the young people the following questions:

- What are some lessons the world has learned from young people?

- Can you think of young athletes or celebrities who have taught powerful lessons to others? What about not-so-famous young people? What about the people with whom you live and go to school with? What lessons have these people taught you?

The Prince of Egypt

DreamWorks SKG, 1998, Rated A-II and PG

SUGGESTED USE: Prayer

MATERIALS: This film clip requires just your basic setup, plus a Bible, a sheet of newsprint, and a marker.

THEMES: Vocation, Leadership, Responding to God's Call, Discernment

LENGTH OF CLIP: 06:33

▶ **Begin:** Chapter 15, 0:42:07 Begin as Moses kisses his wife good-bye.

◼ **End:** 0:48:40 End as Moses tells his wife about his encounter with God.

Setting the Scene

A wonderful version of the call of Moses, this scene can be used for leadership training, a discussion about vocations, or even a conversation about Confirmation. Moses challenges God on his choice of prophets and asks God, "Who am I to lead these people?" This is an attitude shared by us all at various times in our lives. In the end, though, Moses accepts God's challenge to guide the people of Israel, knowing God will help him become a great leader.

Suggested Process

 Show Clip

Discussion Questions

Read the biblical version of this scene in Exodus, chapter 3, aloud to the young people. Then ask the following questions:

- It is only when Moses pays attention to the flame that he hears the voice of God. Where are the burning bushes around you? How is God speaking to you today?

- Perhaps the most haunting phrase in this scene is when God says, "And so, unto Pharoah, I shall send You." Where is God calling you to go today?

- At first Moses says that God has made a mistake. God responds with a question of his own. What does this exchange teach you about the power of God?

- How will God help you do what you are being called to do? How are you already prepared? What preparation do you still need? [Write down the young people's answers on a sheet of newsprint so you can incorporate their responses in to the closing prayer.]

 ## Prayer

Gather the young people in a circle and close by asking for God's blessing on the young people and the needs of the group. Use the newsprint list to incorporate the young people's responses regarding the preparation they need to do what God is calling them to do. Conclude with the Lord's Prayer.

 ## Variation

This scene can be used as part of leadership training. Ask the young people how many different leadership traits they see in Moses. Compare Moses's reaction to God to the young people's initial responses to their own call to leadership.

 ## Final Thought

Moses stands upon holy ground because the presence of God surrounds him. Ask the young people the following questions:

- Where is your sacred space?

- Where do you go to "remove your sandals" and be connected to God?

The Sandlot

Twentieth Century Fox, 1993, Rated A-II and PG

SUGGESTED USE: Conversation Starter

MATERIALS: This film clip requires just your basic setup.

THEMES: Acceptance, Baptism, Peer Pressure, Teamwork

LENGTH OF CLIP: 08:30

▶	**Begin:**	Chapter 6, 0:13:40	Begin as Scotty sits on his front step playing with his glove.
⏹	**End:**	0:22:10	End after Scotty catches the ball and throws it toward the infield, and the others react.

Setting the Scene

The Sandlot is a great film about childhood, teamwork, and friendship, and this clip beautifully captures what so many kids struggle with: being accepted when they feel out of place. Scott Smalls does not know baseball but really wants to fit in with his peers, who live and breathe baseball. Once he makes a catch, he is accepted by the team and so begins a summer filled with adventures.

Use this clip when the young people are not getting along or at the beginning of a sports season to show that all members of the team are important.

Suggested Process

 Show Clip

Discussion Questions

- It is clear that Scotty does not know who Babe Ruth is, so he lies. When do teens sometimes lie so that they are not laughed at by others?

- What is significant about the others kids' spitting on the ground after Benny introduces Scotty?

- Why does Benny defend Scotty when the others are talking about him? Doesn't he risk being made fun of by defending him?

- Have you ever been willing to defend the weaker member of the team or class even if it means being made fun of yourself?

- Once Scotty makes a catch and throws the ball back to the others, he is accepted as part of the team. Have you ever felt like an outsider like Scotty? What was the turning point for you? Was there a leader like Benny who helped introduce you to the rest of the group?

 Variation

The inclusion of Baptism as a theme for this clip may be surprising to some. It is included because the spitting when Scotty is introduced is very much a ritual among the boys. It is almost their way of accepting Scotty, whom Benny has brought to the group, even if the boys are not so sure they are ready to accept him as part of the team. Use that reference as a jumping-off point to talk about Baptism and its implications for those who receive it. Ask the young people the following questions:

- Is it enough to take part in the ritual, or do you still have to "catch the ball" to play the game?

- Is there more required than just showing up?

 Final Thought

Everyone who survived junior high can relate to this film. Everyone who could not catch a ball cringes when Scotty is first introduced to the team. Be sensitive to your audience when using this clip. Are there bullies? Are their victims? Where do you fall on that spectrum? Is there a story from your junior-high experience that you could share with the participants? Is there a person in your past that fell victim to the kind of behavior that makes Scotty feel inferior at the start of this film? Share that story with the young people and let them know they are not alone.

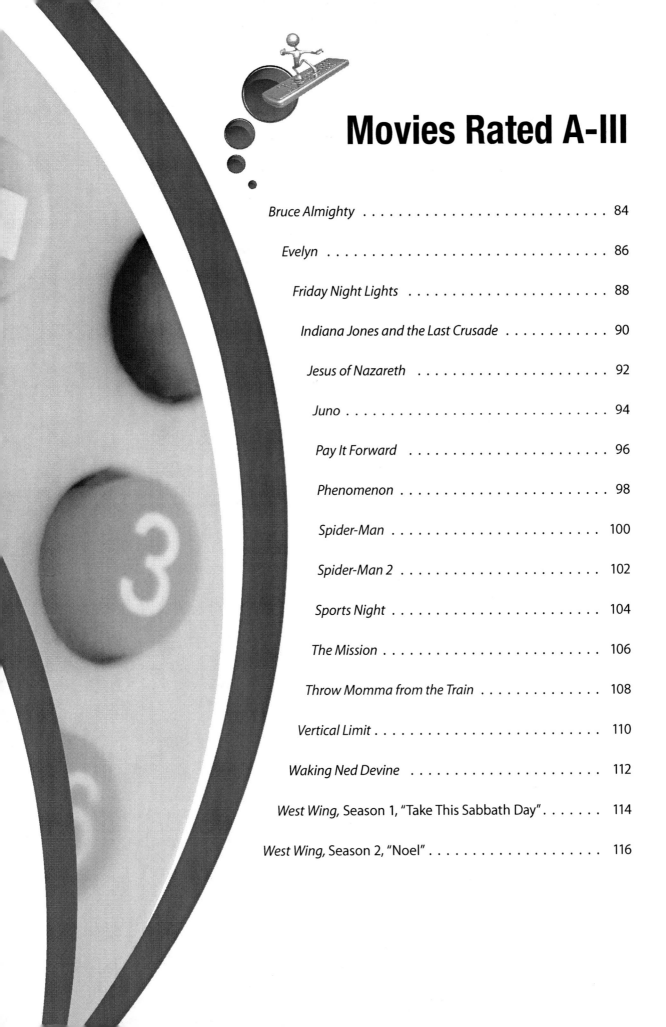

Movies Rated A-III

Bruce Almighty

Universal, 2003, Rated A-III and PG-13

SUGGESTED USE: Prayer

MATERIALS: This film clip requires just your basic setup.

THEMES: Prayer, The Will of God, Surrender, Grace, Selflessness

LENGTH OF CLIP: 05:44

> ▶ **Begin:** Chapter 17, 1:23:36   Begin as Grace's sister opens the door and starts talking to Bruce.
>
> ⬛ **End:**   1:29:20   End when the paramedic says, "We have a pulse."

Setting the Scene

What happens when an arrogant, selfish, man is endowed with all the powers of God? He serves his own needs first. This clip comes when Bruce realizes power isn't really power until you use it for good. In this scene, Bruce surenders to God's will—a challenge for all of us—and lets God be God once again. Pay particular attention to Bruce's prayer.

Suggested Process

 Show Clip

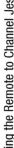

Discussion Questions

- What would you do if you were given all the power of God?

- By this point in the movie, Bruce has messed up just about everything, including his relationship with Grace. Why do failed relationships often leave people so empty?

- What's the first thing you want God to say to you when you meet God in heaven?

- Why does God criticize Bruce's prayer at first? Did Bruce's first prayer sound familiar? Do you ever pray like that?

- Do you think it offends God when we pray with a list of things we want God to do for us? If we could hear God's answer out loud, what do you think God would say to us about such prayers?

 Prayer

Ask the young people to think about the ways they usually pray. Then invite them to imagine themselves in a conversation with God. Ask the following questions:

- How do you think God would respond to your prayer?

- What advice would God give for making your prayer better?

- Think about Bruce's prayer before God. Who are the people in your life you need to see, as Bruce now sees Grace, through the eyes of God?

- What is your prayer for those people? How can your prayer help those people?

- How does this prayer help us?

Spend some time in silence thinking about the obstacles you might need to overcome to see with the eyes of God all those you encounter.

 Variation

We are taught that God always hears our prayers and that God always answers our prayers. Sometimes God says, "I have a better idea." It is in getting used to that "better idea" that we struggle. Use this clip at a time when the students are struggling with God's answer to prayer—for instance, when many have prayed for someone to overcome an illness and the person died anyway. Did God say no, as many believe, or did God heal the person in a way we never imagined?

 Final Thought

It is pretty neat that the name of Bruce's girlfriend is Grace, which means "sharing in God's own life." It is only when Bruce sees Grace through the eyes of God that he is able to really understand what life is all about. What a great message that is for all of us: share in God's life and we will more fully understand our own.

Evelyn

MGM, 2002, Rated A-III and PG

SUGGESTED USE: Prayer

MATERIALS: This film clip requires just your basic setup.

THEMES: Prayer, Family, Reconciliation, Love, Redemption

LENGTH OF CLIPS: 07:52 and 04:51

> ▶ **Begin:** Chapter 25, 1:13:48   Begin as Desmond Doyle testifies.
>
> ⏹ **End:** 1:16:45 or 1:21:40 (for the entire clip)   End when people in court start patting Desmond on the back.
>
> ▶ **Begin:** Chapter 26, 1:16:45   Begin as Evelyn prays.
>
> ⏹ **End:** 1:21:36   End when people in court start patting Desmond on the back.

Setting the Scene

It is 1950s Ireland, when the law forbids a single parent from raising his children alone. Desmond Doyle's sons have been shipped off to a monastary, and his daughter to a convent. Desmond takes on the legal system and fights, all the way to the Supreme Court, to get his children back. The true story of how a father's love for his children changed the law of the land provides us with a scene that allows us to talk about our own families as reflections of God's love.

Split the scene between chapters 25 and 26 (Desmond's testimony and Evelyn's prayer). Use the first chapter as a conversation starter with the discussion questions as a guide. Use the latter to offer a prayer that, like Evelyn's, is both pure and holy.

Suggested Process

 Show Clip (Chapter 25, Desmond's Testimony)

Discussion Questions

- The lawyer tells Desmond that the model for the traditional family is the Holy Family. Do you agree? What do you think of Desmond's response?

- How is the Trinity present in your life today? What effect does it—using Desmond's (and the Scriptures') definition—have on your relationships?

- Earlier in the film, Sister Brigid testified that Evelyn had fallen and that she had not hit Evelyn. What convinces the court that Sister Brigid was lying?

- Why is Evelyn more believable than her father? Why does the lawyer have such a hard time believing that Evelyn prayed for Sister Brigid?

- Evelyn tells the judge she isn't alone, because her grandfather is here with her. Have you ever drawn strength from someone who was with you only in spirit?

 Show Clip (Chapter 26, Evelyn's Prayer)

 Prayer

Invite the young people to think about the people they have offended or hurt, and encourage them to pray for God's forgiveness. Allow a minute or two for silent prayer. Then invite the young people to think about those who have wronged them, and encourage the young people to ask God for the strength to forgive those people. Conclude by reading aloud Matthew 5:44 ("Love your enemies") and allow time for the young people to reflect on the Scripture reading before closing.

 Final Thought

Invite the young people to share the ways their parents seek to build a home rooted in love, filled with hope, and guided by the Holy Spirit.

Friday Night Lights

Imagine Entertainment, 2004, Rated A-III and PG-13

SUGGESTED USE: Conversation Starter

MATERIALS: This film clip requires just your basic setup.

THEMES: Sportsmanship, Teamwork, Leadership, Friendship

LENGTH OF CLIP: 04:29

> ▶ **Begin:** Chapter 27, 1:27:41 Begin at halftime when the coaches are yelling at the players.
>
> ⏹ **End:** 1:32:10 End as the Lord's Prayer concludes.

Setting the Scene

In the economically depressed town of Odessa, Texas, football is king. On Friday nights, there is only one place to be: the local high school stadium. It is the last game of the year—the state championship—and we pick up the scene at halftime. It does not really matter who is winning the game at this point. Pay attention, instead, to the coach's comments about his team.

Use this clip as a way to discuss sportsmanship, teamwork, or even positive leadership skills. The coach does not yell, he does not scream, nor does he use foul language. Still, he inspires. Therein lies a lesson for all those called to lead.

Suggested Process

 Show Clip

Discussion Questions

- What are the different ways the various coaches in this scene try to encourage the athletes? Which ones do you think are most effective?

- Coach Gaines says that being perfect is not about the score. Why is that such a unique vision for a football coach to take? Have you ever had a coach like that?

- The coach says that being perfect is about your relationship with yourself, your family, and your friends. As a Catholic, would it make sense to add God to that list? What would that mean for the other relationships? What would make your relationship with God perfect?

- Why does the coach say his heart is full? What do you think he means? What does it take to make your heart full?

 Variations

Use Jesus's prohibition of oaths in Matthew 5:18–48 to wrap up this session. Pay particular attention to verse 48 ("Be perfect, therefore, as your heavenly Father is perfect."). Challenge the young people to talk about what Jesus meant by that admonition to his followers. What was Jesus coaching his followers to do with this chapter and, in particular, this statement?

 Final Thought

Ask the young people the following questions:

- Can you think of a coach or a teacher who has inspired you? What was so inspiring about the way he or she taught or spoke?

- How are you called to inspire others with your words and actions? What have you done today that has inspired others?

Indiana Jones and the Last Crusade

Paramount, 1989, Rated A-III and PG-13

SUGGESTED USE: Activity

MATERIALS: This film clip requires just your basic setup, plus a sticky note and a pen or pencil for each young person, a blank wall, and a roll of tape (if your notes are not very sticky).

THEMES: Surrender, Following Directions

LENGTH OF CLIP: 04:26

> ▶ **Begin:** Chapter 34, 1:53:51   Begin as Indiana chooses the cup of Christ and rushes back to his father.

> ⏹ **End:** 1:58:17   End as Indiana's father looks back one last time at the Knight.

Setting the Scene

It was the "Last Crusade" for nearly twenty years until the next installment of this series came out, but it is still one of the best in the series. It shows a classic junior-high scene that plays out in classrooms, in homes, and on playgrounds every day. Having just seen what happens to Elsa, Indiana makes the same attempt to get the cup. He hasn't learned anything from her demise and is nearly killed in the process. It is only when his father takes his hand and calls him by name that Indiana hears, understands, and lives.

Use this scene at the end of a school year or at a particularly difficult time in the lives of young people.

Suggested Process

 Show Clip

Discussion Questions

- The cup clearly has healing powers. How, then, do you explain the reaction of fear from so many in this scene?

- Indiana knows that the cup can never cross the great seal, and he has seen what happens to Elsa. So why do you think he still tries to get the cup?

- All through the movie, Indiana's father has been refusing to call him Indiana. He says that was the dog's name and his son's real name is Henry. Knowing that, what is so special about the way Indiana's father speaks to him at the end?

- Why do you think Indiana hears his father's instruction to "let it go"? What are the implications of those words for you in your life right now?

 Activity

Distribute the sticky notes and the pens or pencils to the young people and then offer the following directions:

- Using the backside of the sticky note you have been given, write down one or two things you need to "let go" of. Think in terms of obstacles that are keeping you from a closer relationship with Christ.

- When you are finished, post the sticky note on the blank wall (or other designated space). As you walk away from your note, imagine yourself literally letting go of that obstacle you identified.

 Variation

Set the scene carefully and after the activity is complete, read a few of the young people's sticky notes out loud. Know your audience well enough to know which notes to skip and which to highlight. This can be a great activity during an eighth-grade retreat or for a group of young people or adults who have recently been at odds.

 Final Thought

Invite the young people to think about who pulls them back from the edge when they need saving from their own blindness, foolishness, or arrogance.

Jesus of Nazareth

Artisan, 1977, Rated NR and NR

SUGGESTED USE: Activity

MATERIALS: This film clip requires just your basic setup, plus several index cards and a pen or pencil for each young person.

THEMES: Prayer, Relationships, Faith, Trust, Taking Risks

LENGTH OF CLIP: 04:38

▶ **Begin:** Chapter 37, 2:05:14   Begin as Matthew enters the house of Peter.

◻ **End:**   2:09:52   End as the scene fades to black.

Setting the Scene

This 1977 film is too long for classroom use. Even watching it at home would take a week of evening viewing. It does, however, provide several powerful scenes as told through the eyes of the writers of the Gospels according to Matthew and Mark. In this scene, Jesus has accepted an invitation to visit Peter at his home. The crowds are enormous, and as Jesus teaches about the breaking in of the Reign of God, Matthew the tax collector enters. Invite the young people to watch the scene carefully. It is a story they have surely heard countless times, but it may be the first time they have seen it acted out. Ask the first few questions to begin the process.

Suggested Process

Show Clip

Discussion Questions

- Why were the crowds so concered with Jesus's forgiveness of the man's sins? Why do you think they called him insane?

- Who are the heroes in this scene? [Note: Don't move too quickly through this part of the discussion. Pick a different character and ask why each might be considered heroic. Matthew was willing to go where he was unwanted. The paralytic had the faith to get up when instructed. Jesus cured the man. Peter opened his home to the crowds. Eventually you get to the men who carried their friend to Jesus. Though this is where you want to end up, try taking the long way around the question to help the participants see the bigger picture.]

- Why were the friends heroes just for carrying someone? If they are heroes, why do you think the writers of the Gospels largely ignore them?

 ## Activity

Distribute several index card and a pen or pencil to each young person. Then offer the following directions:

- Think about who carries you to Christ? When you are on the mat, paralyzed by life, by fear, by all the things that weigh you down, who lifts your mat and takes you to the One that gives new life? Write the names of those people on your cards. When you are finished, put the cards away.

 ## Variations

In situations where students may not be getting along in the group or the class, try this activity with one variation: tell the students they cannot list family members on their cards. For an even a bigger challenge, have the young people choose group members. Another variation is to have the young people list the people they have carried to Christ.

 ## Final Thought

Invite the young people to keep their cards in their wallets or purses and to look at them the next time they need a lift. When you meet as a group and things get difficult, remind the young people about their cards.

Juno

Fox Searchlight, 2007, Rated A-III and PG-13

SUGGESTED USE: Conversation Starter

MATERIALS: This film clip requires just your basic setup.

THEMES: Teen Pregnancy, Parent-Child Relationship, Step-Parents, Moral Decision Making

LENGTH OF CLIP: 04:10

 Begin: Chapter 8, 0:22:49   Begin as Juno paces back and forth.

End: 0:26:59   End when Juno's dad says, "Yeah."

Setting the Scene

This film received acclaim for its pro-life message and criticism for its view of teen sexuality. Without glorifying the sexual activity of teenagers, it is possible to show clips from this film that foster healthy discussion about the choices teens make.

In this scene, Juno has to tell her parents she is pregnant. Use this opportunity to talk with the young people about how they would break the news to their parents, but also guide the discussion to what we understand as Catholics to be the reasons sex is saved for marriage. This might be the first time some young people have heard these reasons.

Suggested Process

Show Clip

Discussion Questions

- What do you think of the reaction of Juno's dad and stepmother? How would you tell your parents? How do you think they would react?

- What do you think most frightened Juno in this scene? Would that be the same fear for you?

- Do you admire Juno for her decision to carry the baby to term? What do you think your friends would say if you were pregnant? How would your school, parish, and extended family react?

- Juno's dad says, "I thought you were the kind of girl who knew when to say when." Juno responds, "I don't really know what kind of girl I am." What do you think she means by that? Do you know what kind of girl or boy you are? If not, when and how do you think you will discover that?

 ## Variation

Try to find the statistics for teen pregnancies in your community. See if the young people can guess those statistics. Are they surprised? Gently guide the conversation toward the nature of their decision making and away from topics like abortion or birth control. Know why we believe what we believe and do not pontificate. Young people may respond poorly if they think you are using this scene as an opportunity to preach.

 ## Final Thought

Juno's stepmother says, "Someone is going to find a precious blessing from Jesus in the garbage dump of a situation." How does God right our wrongs? Note that the "wrong" here is having sex. How do we help young people understand that sexuality is a gift to be shared appropriately? Think about all the gifts God gives us and the appropriate and inappropriate ways to use these gifts.

Pay It Forward

Warner Brothers, 2000, Rated A-III and PG-13

SUGGESTED USE: Conversation Starter

MATERIALS: This film clip requires just your basic set up.

THEMES: Expectations, Responsibility, Accepting a Challenge, Faith, Our Role in the Church

LENGTH OF CLIP: 04:50

▶ **Begin:**   Chapter 3, 0:07:34   Begin as Mr. Simonet says, "Now."

◼ **End:**   0:12:24   End as Trevor looks at the board and dreams.

Setting the Scene

A powerful film—and a powerful parable—*Pay It Forward* depicts little Trevor's taking his teacher's challenge to heart and finding a way to change the world.

Use this scene to talk about what the world expects from young people. Then bring it closer to home. What does the Church, their parish, and their families expect of young people? What do you expect from them? If they have seen this film, they know that Trevor's kindness costs him his life. Leave that part of the discussion for another time. This scene is about expectations and accepting a challenge.

Suggested Process

 Show Clip

Discussion Questions

- What does the world expect of you as a teenager? What does the Church expect of you?
- What do you expect of the Church?
- What are the misconceptions about young people and their faith? What would you like adult leaders in the Church and community to know about you and your faith?
- How can the adults in the community support you?

 ## Variation

Invite the young people to take Mr. Simonet's challenge. Ask the young people to come up with one idea that could change the world that they could put into action as a group. Invite them to think locally for a minute. What could they do to change their world? their parish? their school? Is that a more attainable goal?

 ## Final Thought

Is it possible in a world that sometimes values fast food over a home-cooked meal, recreation over hard work, and virtual relationships over meaningful conversations to even imagine what it would be like for one person to make such a big difference? And yet, lone individuals have started movements, made powerful speeches, changed history, and even saved humanity. What role will you play? How will you change the world in your lifetime?

Phenomenon

Touchstone Pictures, 1996, Rated A-III and PG

SUGGESTED USE: Conversation Starter

MATERIALS: This film clip requires just your basic setup, plus a sheet of newsprint and markers for the session variation.

THEMES: The Eucharist, Love, Relationships

LENGTH OF CLIP: 02:31

▶ **Begin:** Chapter 16, 1:44:43   Begin as George is eating an apple while Al and Glory are working on the car.

◼ **End:** 1:47:14   End as the car pulls down the driveway.

Setting the Scene

How can eating an apple be a sign of the Eucharist? Earlier in this film, George reported seeing a bright light. Since then he has had remarkable powers. He can read twenty books in a week, learn a new language in 20 minutes, move objects with his mind—all of which make others think he's crazy. By this point in the film, we realize that these powers are the result of a brain tumor that is stimulating George's brain. He has returned to the home of his girlfriend to die and speaks to her children. In this scene, we discover the truth: we become what we receive. If it is true of the apple (or peanut butter and jelly or pizza or ice cream or anything else), it is true of Holy Communion.

Use this clip as a way to introduce the young people to a new understanding of the sacrament of Holy Communion and its implications for our lives.

Suggested Process

 Show Clip

Discussion Questions

- Why do you think Al and Glory are so quick to run when George admits he has come home to die?

- George tells the children that if he puts the apple down, it will go bad, but if he eats it, it will become a part of him and he can take it with him wherever he goes. Have you ever been told things about the food you eat—that bread crust makes your hair curly, spinach makes you stronger, carrots help your eyesight? Do you think those things are true? What if you never ate any of those foods?

- What do you think George means by the statement, "Everything is on its way somewhere"? Why do you think George's saying this encourages Al to take a bite of the apple?

- If we become what we receive at the dinner table, which certainly encourages healthy eating, is the same thing not true for what happens at the altar on Sunday?

- If we do, in fact, become what we receive from taking part in the Eucharistic celebration on Sundays, what are the implications of that for the rest of our lives? What is now required of us if we have become the Body and Blood of Christ?

 Variation

Make a list of the things your mother and father taught you about what you eat. If you are old enough, recall the commercials from Saturday morning where the piece of broccoli or fruit sang that "we are what we eat." Use these examples to further illustrate the point that we become what we receive. Use newsprint and markers to make a list of the implications of becoming what we receive at Mass for our daily lives.

 Final Thought

If, by sharing in the Eucharistic feast, we become the Body and Blood of Jesus Christ, why is it so hard to act like Christ when Mass is over and we all go home?

Spider-Man

Columbia, 2002, Rated A-III and PG-13

SUGGESTED USE: Activity

MATERIALS: This film clip requires just your basic setup, plus several index cards and a pen or pencil for each young person.

THEMES: Parent-Child Relationships, Courage, Responsibility, Growing Up

LENGTH OF CLIP: 02:00

▶ **Begin:** Chapter 9, 0:34:33 Begin as Uncle Ben and Peter drive down the road.

⏹ **End:** 0:36:33 End as Peter watches Uncle Ben's car turn the corner.

Setting the Scene

This blockbuster provides countless scenes on personal responsibility, family life, and love. This scene, repeated in a flashback in future installments of the films, has Peter's uncle trying to confront Peter on the issue he will face growing up. There are two great lines in this clip, highlighted in the discussion questions. Both of these lines serve as a launchpad for the session activity.

Suggested Process

 Show Clip

Discussion Questions

- Uncle Ben tells Peter that growing up can be difficult and that "now is the time young men change into the man you'll become for the rest of your life." The same holds true for girls. Why can high school be so difficult for young people? Do you think your parents really understand what you go through?

- Uncle Ben tells Peter, "Be careful who you change into." What do you think you can do to prevent growing up into the wrong person? How do decisions you make now affect who you will grow up to become?

- Peter had recently gotten into a fight at school and, as Uncle Ben says, "probably deserved what he got." Uncle Ben also says that just because Peter could beat this guy up, he does not have the right to beat him up. What kind of decisions are you faced with where you are able to do something but do not have the right to do it?

 # Activity

Distribute several index cards and a pen or pencil to each young person. Then offer the following directions:

- Peter hears his uncle say, "Remember, with great power, comes great responsibility." Use the index cards to list the powers you have. Do not overthink this. We all have more power than we realize. Next to each power you list, jot down one or two responsibilities that come with that power.

Invite volunteers to share their lists with the group.

 # Variations

Invite the young people to think more globally. Ask them the following questions:

- Who are the powerful people in your community, in the nation, in the world?
- What responsibilities come with that power?
- Are these powerful people being responsible? If not, what should change?
- Can you change anything locally with the power you have? What responsibilities do you have to make changes?

If you have time, explore Peter's final comments to his uncle and how badly they seem to hurt Uncle Ben. Ask the young people to think about how often we react verbally, ultimately hurting other people. Let the young people know that this scene is the last time Peter sees his uncle Ben. Uncle Ben is carjacked and killed in a later scene while waiting for Peter, who is not studying at the library like he said he would be.

 # Final Thought

This is a powerful scene for a number of reasons. It shows an adolescent being tortured by the pains of growing up and of changing in unexpected ways. Though none of us become Spider-Man, we all experience change in our lives. This scene explores the challenges of growing up, taking responsibility for our actions, and using our God-given power wisely.

Spider-Man 2

Columbia, 2004, Rated A-III and PG-13

SUGGESTED USE: Activity

For this activity, you will need to invite a couple representatives from various fields of ministry to talk to the young people about vocations.

MATERIALS: This film clip requires just your basic setup, plus an index card and a pen or pencil for each young person.

THEMES: Vocation, Choices, Responsibility, Moral Decision Making

LENGTH OF CLIP: 03:33

> ▶ **Begin:** Chapter 26, 0:59:58   Begin as Peter opens his mouth for the doctor.
>
> ◼ **End:**   1:03:31   End when Peter dumps his costume in the trash.

Setting the Scene

Repeating a scene from the first movie in the series, this scene shows Peter going to the doctor to get some advice. He is losing his powers, and the doctor reminds him that he has a choice. Peter follows the doctor's advice and chooses to be "Spider-Man no more."

Use this scene to talk about the advice of the doctor and the choices we have in terms of the person we choose to become.

Suggested Process

 Show Clip

Discussion Questions

- What do you think of the doctor's advice? What do you think he means when he says, "Nothing's as bad as uncertainty"? Have you ever struggled with who you are or with what God's plan is for your life?

- Everyone has a vocation. Some are called to ministry as priests or as men and women religious, some are called to be single, some are called to be married. What do you believe your calling is? How is God preparing you to become that person?

- In a flashback, Uncle Ben tells Peter that he had depended on Peter to take his dreams of honesty, fairness, and justice out into the world. Do you think it is fair to ask others to fulfill a dream of yours? Why do you think Peter would resist noble dreams like these?

- Peter decides to be "Spider-Man no more" and drops his costume—his identity—in the garbage. Have you ever felt like this? Have you ever stopped wanting to be somebody (perhaps someone you felt you needed to be) in favor of being something, or someone, else?

 ## Activity

Invite a couple of representatives from various fields of ministry to be present for this scene. After the clip, have them talk to the young people about what it is like to be a priest or bishop, a sister or brother, a businessperson or youth minister, a dad or a mom. Vocations surround us every day. Do not limit yourself—or the young people—by thinking that vocation always involves a collar or habit.

 ## Final Thought

Peter is told by the doctor that we always have a choice. Is that correct? Do we have a choice? God invites, we respond: one choice. God gives us gifts, we decide how to use them: another choice. God allows us to discover how to use our gifts to serve God: another choice. Life is filled with choices, and it is never too early to help young people understand how to appropriately discern how we make those choices.

Sports Night

Buena Vista, 1998, Rated NR and NR

SUGGESTED USE: Prayer

MATERIALS: This clip requires just your basic setup, plus an index card and a pen or pencil for each young person and a small basket for collecting the cards.

THEMES: Drugs, Sibling Relationships, Reconciliation, Friendship

LENGTH OF CLIP: 22:00

▶ **Begin:** Chapter 2, 0:00:00   Begin with episode 2, "The Apology."

■ **End:** 0:22:00   End when the episode ends.

Setting the Scene

This critically acclaimed television show ran on ABC for two seasons, from 1998 to 2000, and tells the story of how a television sports show is put together. In this episode, which originally aired on September 29, 1998, one of the main characters, Dan Rydell, is the subject of an article in *Esquire* magazine. One of his quotes is taken out of context and leads the CEO of the network to believe Dan supports the legalization of marijuana. Demanding an on-air apology, the network gets more than they bargained for when they hear what Dan has to say.

Use this scene to talk about the effects of drug use on those we love, the relationships among siblings, and the various forms reconciliation can take.

Suggested Process

 Show Clip

Discussion Questions

- Dan says that those who are lucky enough to be the subject of magazine articles have an obligation to raise the level of debate. Do you think that is true? Why? What responsibilities do celebrities have toward those who are not famous?

- Why do you think Isaac is so eager for Dan to apologize and then move on? Do you agree with his telling Dan that an apology is necessary? Have you ever had to apologize for something because someone misinterpreted what you said or did?

- Were you surprised by Dan's apology? Why do you think he finally told that story, which was clearly a surprise to his coworkers? Do you think his apology satisfied the network executives?

 ## Prayer

Gather the young people into a circle and distribute the index cards and pens or pencils. Place the basket in the center of the circle. Then give the following directions:

- Think of some things for which you need to apologize. Have you done something, or failed to do something, that has had an adverse effect on others? Are there times when you failed to be a positive influence on others? Use your index card to make a list of all the things you want to apologize for. Next to each item list the name or names of the person or people you need to apologize to.

- When you are finished, fold your index card in half and place it in the basket.

Lead the group in a prayer of reconciliation. Afterward invite the young people to think about these questions:

- What needs to happen in order for you to be reconciled with those on your list?

- What needs to happen in order for you to be reconciled with God?

 ## Variation

Pause the episode before Dan and Casey go on the air, and ask the young people whether they believe Dan should have to apologize. Talk about the need for admitting when you are wrong, even if your apology is only because of the way others have interpreted the situation. Talk about why that can be so difficult.

 ## Final Thought

Conclude with the sign of peace.

The Mission

Warner Brothers, 1986, Rated A-III and PG

Suggested Use: Conversation Starter

Materials: This film clip requires just your basic setup.

Themes: Penance, Suffering, Redemption, Mercy

Length of Clip: 14:37

> ▶ **Begin:**   Chapter 9, 0:27:50   Begin as Father Gabriel walks toward the prison.
>
> ⏹ **End:**   0:42:27   End as the music plays and Rodrigo cries.

Setting the Scene

An epic tale of a darker period of Church history, this film tells the story of two unlikely allies who team up to save a tribe of Native South American Indians from the colonial powers that want their land. Slave trader Rodrigo Mendoza killed his brother. In this scene, missionary Father Gabriel offers him a chance at redemption. For his penance, he must carry, on his own, the supplies to the mission above the falls. It is a difficult scene to watch. Perhaps because the supplies are heavy. Perhaps because it reminds us all of our own baggage.

Use this clip as a conversation starter about penance and the need for God's forgiveness.

Suggested Process

 Show Clip

Discussion Questions

- Rodrigo loved his brother and yet killed him in a sword fight over a woman. He believes that God will never forgive him and that there is no penance that can bring redemption. Do you think there are crimes that are unforgivable? Is it possible to put yourself beyond God's love?

- Father Gabriel asks if Rodrigo is willing to take a chance on penance. Rodrigo responds, "Are you ready to see it fail?" Do you think it is possible for a penance to fail?

- Though it's never spoken, we know the penance Father Gabriel gives Rodrigo is to carry the pack up to the mission above the falls. What you also need to know is that Rodrigo was a slave trader who imprisoned some of the Indians in the mission. Why does this make the penance more difficult? Why do you think Father offered this penance instead of some alternative?

- At one point, Father John approaches Father Gabriel and says that he and the other brothers believe Rodrigo has done this penance long enough. Are you surprised at Father Gabriel's answer? Why do you think Rodrigo keeps going?

- When Rodrigo finally makes it to the top, one of the Indians cuts the pack of supplies and pushes it down the embankment. Why is this significant? Why not keep the supplies? Why do the Indians laugh at him? How did you feel when they cut the pack away?

 Variation

- The children raise an alarm with the elders of the community when they see Rodrigo coming up the hill with the supplies. We cannot understand what the child who wields the knife says, but we can guess it must have something to do with Rodrigo's past. After the young people have viewed the scene, have them think about what the Indians are saying considering Rodrigo's reaction. Replay the last few minutes of the scene and let the young people talk over the native language, filling in the conversation as they imagine it. Play the scene without the sound. Write down or share their ideas.

 Final Thought

We all carry the burden of someone else's reputation or sense of self-worth in our hands each day. What we say about others says a great deal about us. What are your words revealing today about the environment you are creating for yourself, your family, your future?

Throw Momma from the Train

MGM, 1987, Rated A-III and PG-13

SUGGESTED USE: Conversation Starter

MATERIALS: This film clip requires just your basic setup.

THEMES: Confirmation, Finding Meaning, Relationships

LENGTH OF CLIP: 03:50

▶ **Begin:** Chapter 10, 0:48:59 Begin as Owen brings the eggs to the table.

⬛ **End:** 0:52:49 End as Owen says, "Thanks, Larry."

Setting the Scene

This dark comedy about a momma's boy who wants to end his mother's life contains only the insinuation of violence. Larry is Owen's teacher, and Owen, who is not a very good student, wants Larry's help in becoming a writer. After Larry suggests Owen go see Hitchcock's *Strangers on a Train,* Owen gets the idea that if he kills Larry's ex-wife, who stole a book idea from Larry, then Larry would have to get rid of Owen's mother. After the ex-wife falls off a boat and goes missing, Owen takes credit and tries to convince Larry to kill his mom. In this scene, Larry meets Owen's mother, Owen panics, and then the two share a few moments that set the scene for some powerful conversation about the rituals we experience as Catholic Christians.

Suggested Process

 Show Clip

Discussion Questions

- Why doesn't Larry want to see the coin collection? Why does he relent?

- At first, what is your reaction to the coin collection? When does that change?

- Why are these coins so important to Owen? What does this exchange teach Larry about his student?

- To the person outside the situation (in this case, Larry), the coins mean nothing. Once Larry is invited in, the coins mean so much more. How is that like the water, fire, oil, and laying on of hands we receive at Confirmation? What do those things mean outside the sacrament or to someone not involved? What do they mean to the one who has accepted the invitation to be a part of the story?

- How are we like Larry when he sits in the chair and refuses to see the collection? Are there people in our lives inviting us to be a part of their story and we refuse? How should we be reacting?

 ## Variation

Another way to use this clip is to simply ask, after you have shown it, "Name three or four things you learned from that scene." Then give the young people a chance to name that which they have learned. See if you can bring the conversation around to the act of being invited, responding to the invitation, and what we learn from taking part in the stories of others. This is a simple scene with a powerful message. Larry learns about Owen's relationship with his father and more fully understands Owen's relationship with his mother.

 ## Final Thought

At first we dismissed Owen and his silly coins as just that: silliness ("Here's a nickel . . . a quarter"). As the music began and Owen started speaking about his father, our laughter turned to silence. How could something so small be filled with such powerful memories? Bring something with you when you use this clip—the blanket your grandmother crocheted for you, your dad's class ring, your baptismal candle. How can something so small and insignificant to others mean so much to you? Use this as a moment of spiritual show-and-tell for the rituals and sacramentals in your life.

Vertical Limit

Columbia, 2000, Rated A-III and PG-13

SUGGESTED USE: Conversation Starter

MATERIALS: This film clip requires just your basic setup.

THEMES: Moral Decision Making, Sibling Relationships, Character

LENGTH OF CLIP: 05:28

 Begin: Chapter 2, 0:01:02   Begin immediately after the opening credits, as the eagle flies across the mountain range.

End: 0:06:30   End with the close-up of Peter's face.

Setting the Scene

A tough clip to watch, this scene has a family of rock climbers facing the ultimate challenge. When a couple of sloppy climbers cause them to lose their footing, Peter, Annie, and their father are hanging on for dear life, literally. To save both children, Royce, the father, tells his son, Peter, that Peter has to cut the rope. Doing so will kill Royce but save Peter and Annie. If Peter doesn't cut the rope, they will all die. This scene, and the conversation that follows, can be used to talk about the tough decisions we all face, even if most of them are not a matter of life or death.

Suggested Process

Show Clip

Discussion Questions

- Why do you think Peter and Annie's dad initially seems so calm? Would you have been able to keep your cool? Were you surprised by his command to his son, "I need you to do something for me"? What would you have said if you were the father?

- What would you have done if you were Peter? Could you cut the rope? What if your sister was not present, and you were only going to save yourself? Assume your dad is shouting the same instructions.

- How do you think Annie will react if Peter cuts the rope? How would you react if you were Annie?

- What if the positions on the rope were reversed, and the father was in a position to be saved by cutting the rope? How does that change the argument?

- Have you ever known a parent to willingly sacrifice himself or herself for her or his children? Are all the sacrifices you can think of matters of life and death?

 ## Variation

Let the scene play until we see the decision Peter makes. How does that change the conversation? Were the young people surprised by what happened? Hollywood can make things seem easier, but what are the ramifications for these decisions in real life? Do teenagers face life-or-death decisions? What about teens who are licensed to drive? Take it down a notch or two and talk about the decisions we face that do not involve such grave matters. We may not have to make a life-or-death decision when we are teenagers, but we can help people move closer to heaven, or farther away, depending on our own words and actions.

 ## Final Thought

Ask the young people to try to imagine all the ways parents sacrifice for their children. Many may seem trite—a lack of sleep, a lack of personal space, buying for others instead of themselves. This is part of growing up and becoming responsible adults. How can the young people practice becoming responsible by making good decsions? What do the young people face that requires a decision that either brings them closer to God or farther away? Are any of those decisions a matter of life or death? What about a matter of salvation?

Waking Ned Devine

Twentieth Century Fox, 1996, Rated A-III and PG-13

SUGGESTED USE: Activity

MATERIALS: This film clip requires just your basic setup, plus a sheet of paper and a marker for each young person.

THEMES: Legacy, Friendship, Honesty

LENGTH OF CLIP: 06:08

▶ **Begin:**   Chapter 18, 1:12:31   Begin as the funeral procession is led by the man playing the pennywhistle.

⏹ **End:**   1:18:39   End as the casket is taken from the church.

Setting the Scene

Ned Devine is dead. Too bad he signed the back of the winning lotto ticket before he died. Now Michael has to pretend he is Ned so the townspeople can split the winnings. In this scene, the town is burying Ned and celebrating his funeral. Soon the man from the lotto shows up and instead of eulogizing Ned, Jackie has to talk about his dear friend Michael or the lotto man will figure out what is going on.

Use this scene as a way to introduce an activity that invites the young people to consider what they want others to say about them when they are gone. How will they be remembered?

Suggested Process

 Show Clip

Discussion Questions

- Jackie says that the words that are spoken at a funeral come too late. Are there people in your life you have hesitated to say things to? Do you need to forgive?

- Jackie does not say much, and yet he also says a great deal. What would you want someone to say at your funeral? How would you want to be remembered?

 Activity

Distribute the paper and markers to the young people and then offer the following directions:

- Use the the paper and markers to write your epitaph. What words would describe the life you have led? What legacy do you wish to leave?

 Variation

Use Mark 13:30–33 as a reflection and as a way to remind young people what Jesus said about not knowing the day or the hour of our own death. What does that reading and this scene teach us about the way we should live our lives? How can we be challenged to remember that we are creating our legacies now with the words we say and the way we treat one another?

 Final Thought

"Be careful how you live. You may be the only Bible some people read." This old saying, about the way people will remember us, should not be the only thing motivating us to treat others well. Yet it helps to be reminded that every word, every action, builds our legacy. What will others say about you? How will your memory live on in the lives of others?

West Wing, Season 1, "Take This Sabbath Day"

Warner Brothers Television, 2000, Rated NR and NR

SUGGESTED USE: Conversation Starter

MATERIALS: This clip requires just your basic setup.

THEME: Sanctity of Life, Moral Decision Making, Prayer, Wisdom

LENGTH OF CLIP: 06:48

▶ **Begin:** Chapter 5, 0:36:07   Begin as the snow falls in front of the White House and the words on the screen say "Sunday 11:57 P.M."

⬛ **End:** 0:42:55   End as the scene fades to black.

Setting the Scene

In the first year of his first term, President Bartlet is faced with a life-or-death decision—whether to commute a sentence of a man who is about to be executed. He has to act by midnight but chooses to do nothing. The man is executed about the same time the president's parish priest comes to visit.

Use this scene to lay the groundwork for a lively discussion about the merits of the death penalty. Give the young people a chance to talk about what they would do in President Bartlet's shoes.

Suggested Process

 Show Clip

Discussion Questions

- President Bartlet says he spent the weekend looking for a way out. Father Cavanaugh says that his way out was simple: "Only God gets to kill people." What does this argument do to those who favor the death penalty? What about other life-or-death issues?

- President Bartlet says he prays for wisdom and none comes. Do you believe that God hears our prayers? Does God always answer our prayers?

- There is a bumper sticker that says, "We kill people who kill people to show that killing people is wrong." What do you think the person who wrote the sticker was trying to say? Do you agree? Why?

- Do you think capital punishment is a crime deterrant? If not, why not? Are there other ways to deal with people who commit heinous crimes like murder?

- Have you ever "missed the boat" like President Bartlet did? When have you failed to recognize that God was trying to tell you something only to realize later that you had missed the message?

Variation

Show the beginning of chapter 5 to show what two staff members have to say about why the death penalty is wrong, or should be illegal. The scene also shows President Bartlet's chief of staff giving the him an out. There are added scenes that follow a different story line, but those can easily be ignored. Ask the following questions:

- What do you think about Toby and Sam's thoughts?

- Are you surprised by Leo's advice to leave this issue for the next president to solve?

Final Thought

What kind of world would it be if we all followed the priest's statement that "only God gets to kill people"?

West Wing, Season 2, "Noel"

Warner Brothers Television, 2000, Rated NR and NR

SUGGESTED USE: Activity

MATERIALS: This clip requires just your basic setup, plus a Bible for each small group of three or four for the session activity. For the session variation, you will need a list of common parables, cut into strips, and a hat or bucket to hold the slips.

THEME: Compassion, Friendship, Parables

LENGTH OF CLIP: 09:32

▶ **Begin:** Chapter 5, 0:31:38 Begin as Josh asks the doctor what his diagnosis was.

⏹ **End:** 0:41:10 End after Leo says, "As long as I got a job, you've got a job."

Setting the Scene

In this scene from Aaron Sorkin's Emmy-winning television show, Deputy Chief of Staff Josh Lyman is reminded by his boss what friendship is all about. In the season finale of the first season, Josh was shot. Now he is suffering from post-traumatic stress disorder and has to spend the day with a psychiatrist. He is met by his boss as he leaves his appointment. Surprised that his boss waited for him, Josh listens to Leo's story—a variation on a story we have all heard many times.

Suggested Process

 Show Clip

Discussion Questions

- Josh is afraid to admit (and has spent the episode denying) the truth of how he hurt his hand. He has been telling everyone he broke a glass in his apartment. When he realizes his boss cares enough to wait around for him, he tells the truth. Why are we sometimes afraid to admit we need help?

- Leo tells a story to Josh that parallels the story of the good Samaritan in Luke 10:30–37. What is the lesson of Leo's version?

 ## Activity

Direct the young people to form small groups of three or four. Distribute a Bible to each small group, and then offer the following directions:

- Pick a parable from the Gospels. How would you make it into a modern tale? What lessons would it teach? How would you change it? See which group can be more creative in your revisions of these wonderful stories.

 ## Variation

See if you can have a friendly competition among the small groups. Instead of having the groups choose parables, have a list of the most common ones ready, and let each group draw one out of the hat or bucket. Challenge each group to come up with a lesson that goes beyond their own schools or parishes. Is it possible for them to create a version of the parable that teaches social justice or the sanctity of life?

 ## Final Thought

The purpose of a parable is to invite the one hearing the story into a new understanding of reality. Parables enable us to see things in a new light and then challenge us to live according to that new insight. What new insights can be drawn from the young people's stories? What invitations have been made to live according to those new insights?

Movie Index

▶ By Suggested Use

ACTIVITY

CONVERSATION STARTER

PRAYER

▶ By USCCB Rating

A-I RATING

A-I: GENERAL PATRONAGE. Strictly speaking, this does not simply connote films that are "for" children, or films in which they would necessarily be interested. Rather, any film free from significant objectionable content might receive this classification. In the old Hollywood days, when it was assumed that virtually all mainstream films were acceptable for all audiences, many films with "adult" subject matter, like *Giant,* received this classification. Nowadays, with even the cleanest adult films containing at least one four-letter word, such examples are rare.

A-II RATING

A-II: ADULTS AND ADOLESCENTS. Though a 13-year-old is technically an adolescent, the original intent of this classification was an endorsement for older teens. However, some ambiguity remains in this category, and the Office generally indicates whether the film is most appropriate for "older teens" or anyone over the age of thirteen. Films with nudity, overt sexual activity (even if implied), violence with bloodshed, and use of four-letter words are almost never allowed in the A-I or A-II categories. *Akeelah and the Bee*—an uplifting film about a girl who wins a spelling bee—is one exception. In the film, one schoolmate utters an expletive. Yet, *Akeelah* was deemed so appropriate and inspirational for young viewers, that the movie was classified A-I.

A-III RATING

A-III: ADULTS. This can be a tricky category. Adult sensibilities run the gamut from a cosmopolitan readership with a wider tolerance for edgy subject matter to more sensitive moviegoers who find certain elements less palatable. We try to strike a balance between the two. Oftentimes, a worthy film is clearly "adult" in subject matter, but older teens might derive benefit from it, so a sentence may be added about it being "acceptable" or "possibly acceptable" for "older teens." Dramatically justified violence, moderate sexual content of a "nondeviant" nature, restrained nudity, and valid use of coarse language are permissible here.

NOT RATED (NR)

▶ By Motion Picture Association of America (MPAA) Rating System

G: GENERAL AUDIENCE

PG: PARENTAL GUIDANCE SUGGESTED

▶ By Theme